Methuen Drama Mo[dern]

The Methuen Drama Modern Plays series has always been at the forefront of modern playwriting and has reflected the most exciting developments in modern drama since 1959. To commemorate the fiftieth anniversary of Methuen Drama, the series was relaunched in 2009 as Methuen Drama Modern Classics, and continues to offer readers a choice selection of the best modern plays.

The Lonesome West

Valene and Coleman, two brothers living alone in their father's house after his recent death, find it impossible to exist without the most massive and violent disputes over the most mundane and innocent of topics. Only Father Welsh, the local young priest, is prepared to try to reconcile the two before their petty squabblings spiral into vicious and bloody carnage.

Martin McDonagh's first play, *The Beauty Queen of Leenane*, was the 1996 winner of the George Devine Award, won the Writers' Guild Award for Best Fringe Play and also the *Evening Standard* Award for Most Promising Newcomer. The play was nominated for six Tony awards, of which it won four, and a Laurence Olivier Award (the BBC Award for Best New Play). *The Beauty Queen of Leenane* is the first in Martin McDonagh's *Leenane Trilogy*; *A Skull in Connemara*, which was nominated for an Olivier Award for Best New Comedy, and *The Lonesome West* completed the cycle. His other work includes the plays *The Cripple of Inishmaan*, *The Lieutenant of Inishmore* and *The Pillowman*, and the film script for *In Bruges*.

WITHDRAWN
FROM
STOCK

by the same author

The Beauty Queen of Leenane
A Skull in Connemara
The Cripple of Inishmaan
The Lieutenant of Inishmore

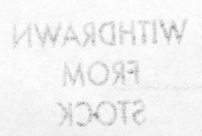

Martin McDonagh

The Lonesome West

Methuen Drama

822 McD   5530416

Methuen Drama Modern Classic

8 10 9

Methuen Drama
A & C Black Publishers Limited
36 Soho Square
London W1D 3QY
www.methuendrama.com

First published in Great Britain in 1997 by Methuen Drama
in association with the Royal Court Theatre

Reissued with additional material and a new cover 2009

Copyright © 1997 by Martin McDonagh
Introduction copyright © 2009 by Methuen Drama

Martin McDonagh has asserted his rights under the Copyright, Designs
and Patents Act 1988 to be identified as the author of this work

ISBN 978 0 413 71980 5

A CIP catalogue record for this book is available
from the British Library

Typeset by Country Setting, Kingsdown, Kent
Printed and bound in Great Britain by Cox & Wyman Ltd,
Reading, Berkshire

Caution

All rights whatsoever in these plays are strictly reserved and
application for performance etc. should be made to the author's agent:
The Rod Hall Agency Ltd, 6th Floor, Fairgate House,
78 New Oxford Street, London WC1A 1HB..
No performance may be given unless a licence has been obtained.

This book is sold subject to the condition that it shall not,
by way of trade or otherwise, be lent, resold, hired out, or otherwise
circulated without the publisher's prior consent in any form of binding
or cover other than that in which it is published and without
a similar condition, including this condition, being imposed
on the subsequent purchaser.

Leabharlann
Contae na Midhe

Introduction

The Lonesome West takes its title from John Millington Synge's 1907 classic, *The Playboy of the Western World*. In that drama, a young man called Christy Mahon famously arrives at a west of Ireland pub, claiming to have killed his father. This story so impresses the pub's owner – the drunken and self-centred Michael James Flaherty – that he instantly offers Christy a job: he will be employed as the pub's pot-boy and will therefore be able to protect Flaherty's daughter Pegeen while the old man spends the night getting drunk at a funeral. This decision prompts an uneasy response from Pegeen's fiancé, the effeminate and priest-fearing Shawn Keogh. Earlier in the play, Flaherty had mocked his future son-in-law. 'Oh, there's sainted glory this day in the lonesome west,' he says to Pegeen, 'and by the will of God I've got you a decent man!' He's being entirely sarcastic here: Shawn's 'saintliness' and 'decency' are regarded as negative rather than admirable traits by Flaherty and his fellow villagers.

It's easy to understand why McDonagh draws on this line for his own play, the final part of a trilogy set in a west of Ireland village called Leenane. For centuries, Ireland's western region has been idealised as a place of stunning natural beauty, rich in traditional culture and folklore. But Synge and McDonagh both show that it's also a place that has been impoverished in many ways – not just economically, but culturally and (perhaps) intellectually also. The West is a wonderful place to visit, they suggest; and it's a wonderful place to write about too – but it doesn't seem to offer much to the people who actually live there. In these plays, those who are ambitious and talented can choose between two options: to emigrate or, as happens more frequently, to surrender to frustration and bitterness. Everyone else gets on with the sad task of surviving from one day to the next. It's little wonder, then, that Synge and McDonagh's most admirable characters feel so isolated, despite being surrounded by countless other people. It is for this reason that the word 'lonesome' and its variants appear thirty-three times in Synge's play, and almost as often in McDonagh's.

Also evident in that line from *The Playboy* is a dangerously
skewed sense of morality. The arrival in Flaherty's pub of a
man who has murdered his father should provoke a negative
response: fear, outrage, a desire to see justice done. Yet as
Flaherty's sarcasm indicates, it is Christy's willingness to be
violent, rather than Shawn's sense of morality, that is seen as a
blessing – as a 'sainted glory' enacted through the 'will of God'.
To Synge's original audience, this line seemed blasphemous.
But what makes these words provocative even now is that they
reveal the disjunction between the appearance and the reality
of religious faith within Irish culture. The language of Synge's
villagers is rich in religious allusion, yet it's also obvious that
they have all failed completely to understand and internalise
the central tenets of Christianity: forgiveness, compassion,
charity, selflessness and, above all, love for others.

Synge's insight about the place of religion in Irish society is
at the heart of *The Lonesome West*, a play that presents Leenane
as a town in which 'God has no jurisdiction'. McDonagh's
uproarious tale about Valene and Coleman, two warring
brothers, may owe much more to the films of the Marx
Brothers than the biblical story of Cain and Abel, but behind
the mayhem, serious questions are being asked. Is it possible
to lead a genuinely good life in modern Ireland? Or should
we see Leenane's moral life as being just like the vol-au-vents
served up at the village's many funerals – firm on the surface,
but empty at the core?

These questions torment the town's priest, the 'maudlin
and lonesome Father Welsh'. They drive him first to drink
and then, as the play moves towards a conclusion, to a
desperate act that seems motivated in equal parts by courage,
stupidity, and Guinness. Welsh's downfall is that he tries
always to see the best in his parishioners. For instance, when
he learns of the suicide of the local policeman Tom Hanlon,
he describes him as a man who 'never had a bad word to say
about anybody and did his best to be serving the community
every day of his life'. Yet the audience – and McDonagh's
characters – know this description is wholly inaccurate.

Hanlon plays a major role in the second of McDonagh's Leenane plays, *A Skull in Connemara*, and is shown there to be vindictive, malicious, and in search of self-advancement at all costs. Welsh, then, is either hopelessly naive or is instead being deliberately dishonest.

And just as Welsh is too kind to Hanlon, he may also be placing too much faith in Valene and Coleman, believing that if he can persuade them to make peace with each other he might just be able to redeem himself – if not in God's eyes, then perhaps in his own. The real tragedy for Welsh, of course, is that he lacks the self-awareness to realise that redemption is available – not through his act of self-sacrifice, but through the love of Girleen, one of the few genuinely likeable characters in McDonagh's *oeuvre*. If Leenane is a kind of hell on earth, driving Welsh to drink and Valene and Coleman to violence, it provokes a different kind of response from Girleen – hope for the future. 'At least when you're still here there's the possibility of happiness,' she tells Welsh, rejecting the suggestion that suicide is the only logical response to a life that seems unbearable. Yet Welsh doesn't realise that the happiness Girleen hopes for is available to him too.

Instead, the priest tries to save Valene and Coleman, mainly because he sees their life as 'sad and lonesome', noting in particular the damaging effects of the absence of women from their lives. There's certainly plenty of evidence that the brothers are sexually frustrated, from Coleman's repeated references to having things shoved 'up his arse', to both men's homophobia, to Valene's response to the claim that Girleen 'groped' his brother ('What did it feel like?' he asks, rather pathetically). Yet McDonagh makes clear that neither man is really interested in the redemption offered by Welsh, who is far more 'sad and lonesome' than they are. 'What's wrong with fighting anyways?' asks Coleman. 'I do like a good fight. It does show you care, fighting does'. 'I *do* like a good fight, the same as that', agrees Valene. The violence between the pair is thus seen as a perverted form of brotherly love, a response to the frustration and isolation both men experience.

Besides, the brothers can turn to religion to justify their actions. 'I'm sure to be getting into heaven,' says Valene, referring not to the way that he lives his life, but instead to his extensive collection of religious figurines. Coleman too is blithely confident of his salvation. 'Me, probably straight to heaven I'll go, even though I blew the head off poor dad. So long as I go to confessing it anyways. That's the great thing about being Catholic. You can shoot your dad in the head and it doesn't even matter at all.'

McDonagh has an obvious interest in familial relations – his first six plays all feature a troubled relationship between two siblings. *The Lonesome West* develops this theme to its fullest extent, drawing not only from Synge but also from the great American play about a battle between two brothers, Sam Shepard's *True West*. Yet although his story has universal resonances, McDonagh's play also has something specific to say about the place of Catholicism in modern Ireland.

The Lonesome West premiered in 1997, at a time when Irish society was just learning of the institutionalised abuse, over many decades, of thousands of the country's most vulnerable citizens by members of the Catholic Church. It's easy to forget that, for many members of McDonagh's first Irish audiences, some of his jokes about Catholicism were extraordinarily provocative. Seeking to reassure Father Welsh, for instance, Coleman says, 'You're a fine priest. Number one you don't go abusing five-year olds, so, sure, doesn't that give you a head-start over half the priests in Ireland?' Later, Valene will describe Welsh as the 'laughing stock of the Catholic Church in Ireland', vindictively adding that this 'takes some fecking doing, boy'. As McDonagh's play progresses, the audience is forced to think about the fact that clerical abuse in Ireland lasted for several decades, and that its impact is evident everywhere: not just in the brothers' twisted sense of morality, but also in their father's strange habit of screaming at nuns.

Perhaps the most pointed moment in the play, then, is a discussion between Father Welsh and Girleen in the fourth scene. Welsh has realised that Leenane is the 'murder capital of fecking Europe'. He knows that Maureen Folan killed her mother (an event described in the first part of the trilogy, *The Beauty Queen of Leenane*), and suspects strongly that Mick Dowd killed his wife (as explored in *A Skull in Connemara*). So the news that Coleman is also responsible for a murder has deeply affected Welsh. But even more shocking to him is that Girleen was aware of these events long before he was – and that she did nothing. 'I think I did hear a rumour somewhere' about the murder, she concedes. 'A fecking rumour?' he replies. 'And you didn't bat an eye or go reporting it?'

This is a key moment in the play. Violence, abuse, and brutality can arise from many causes, but Welsh shows his awareness that good people who do nothing to stop wrong-doing are themselves morally culpable. In 1997, this suggestion resonated with an Irish audience that was slowly realising that clerical child abuse was not simply a result of the Church's covering up of its members' crimes – it was also enabled by a culture of silence that pervaded the entire society. Like Girleen, we in Ireland had for decades heard 'a rumour somewhere' about what was happening and, with only a few exceptions, we did nothing. If McDonagh shows us that Irish Catholicism is (quite literally) in meltdown, he also challenges us to consider how this situation arose in the first place.

Welsh's response thus helps us to understand the play's conclusion. As the lights fade, a spotlight rests for a moment on three objects hanging on the wall centre-stage: a crucifix, a letter by Father Welsh, and a chain bought for him by Girleen. It's clear that these three symbols mean nothing to Valene and Coleman. The crucifix signifies a kind of self-sacrifice that neither man can achieve, the letter is a call for a peace that neither man desires, and the chain is a symbol of the love that neither man will ever experience. Why then does the light linger on this part of the set? Should the audience leave the theatre feeling hopeless, convinced that Valene and Coleman will never change? Perhaps.

But perhaps the purpose of those images is instead to force the audience to think about their own lives, and their own responsibilities. McDonagh's Leenane is of course an imagined location, bearing little resemblance to the real Galway village, just as his dialogue is an exaggerated version of real Irish speech, and his characters an exaggerated version of standard dramatic types. Nevertheless, the dilemmas at the heart of *The Lonesome West* are real enough. Like Synge before him, McDonagh is inviting the audience to consider the difference between appearance and reality, reminding us that *seeming* to be good and *being* good are rarely the same thing. We must, then, leave the theatre facing the question asked so poignantly by Father Welsh and Girleen. When we are confronted with intolerable brutality, what must we do in response? This question was urgent for McDonagh's first audiences in 1997. It remains urgent now – and not just in Ireland's lonesome west.

Patrick Lonergan
Galway, 2009

The Lonesome West

The Lonesome West, a Royal Court and Druid Theatre Company co-production, was first presented as part of 'The Leenane Trilogy' at the Town Hall Theatre, Galway, on 10 June 1997, and subsequently opened at the Royal Court Theatre Downstairs, St Martin's Lane, on 19 July 1997. The cast was as follows:

Girleen Kelleher	Dawn Bradfield
Father Welsh	David Ganly
Coleman Connor	Maelíosa Stafford
Valene Connor	Brían F. O'Byrne

Director Garry Hynes
Designer Francis O'Connor
Lighting Ben Ormerod
Sound Bell Helicopter
Music Paddy Cunneen

Characters

Girleen Kelleher
Father Welsh
Coleman Connor
Valene Connor

Setting

Leenane, a small town in Connemara, County Galway.

Scene One

The kitchen/living room of an old farmhouse in Leenane, Galway. Front door far right, table with two chairs down right, an old fireplace in the centre of the back wall, tattered armchairs to its right and left. Door to **Coleman**'s *room in the left back wall. Door to* **Valene**'s *room far left. A long row of dusty, plastic Catholic figurines, each marked with a black 'V', line a shelf on the back wall, above which hangs a double-barrelled shotgun and above that a large crucifix. A food cupboard on the wall left, a chest of drawers towards the right, upon which rests a framed photo of a black dog. As the play begins it is day.* **Coleman**, *dressed in black, having just attended a funeral, enters, undoing his tie. He takes a biscuit tin out of a cupboard, tears off the Sellotape that binds its lid and takes out from it a bottle of poteen, also marked with a 'V'.* **Father Welsh**, *a thirty-five-year-old priest, enters just behind him.*

Welsh I'll leave the door for Valene.

Coleman Be doing what you like.

He pours two glasses as **Welsh** *sits at the table.*

Coleman You'll have a drink with me you will?

Welsh I will, Coleman, so.

Coleman (*quietly*) A dumb fecking question that was.

Welsh Eh?

Coleman I said a dumb fecking question that was.

Welsh Why, now?

Coleman *gives* **Welsh** *his drink without answering and sits at the table also.*

Welsh Don't be swearing today of all days anyway, Coleman.

Coleman I'll be swearing if I want to be swearing.

Welsh After us only burying your dad, I'm saying.

Coleman Oh aye, right enough, sure you know best, oh aye.

Welsh (*pause*)   Not a bad turnout anyways.

Coleman   A pack of vultures only coming nosing.

Welsh   Come on now, Coleman. They came to pay their last respects.

Coleman   Did seven of them, so, not come up asking where the booze-up after was to be held, and Maryjohnny then 'Will ye be having vol-au-vents?' There'll be no vol-au-vents had in this house for the likes of them. Not while Valene holds the purse-strings anyways. If it was me held the purse-strings I'd say aye, come around for yourselves, even if ye are vultures, but I don't hold the purse-strings. Valene holds the purse-strings.

Welsh   Valene does be a biteen tight with his money.

Coleman   A biteen? He'd steal the shite out of a burning pig, and this is his poteen too, so if he comes in shouting the odds tell him you asked me outright for it. Say you sure enough demanded. That won't be hard to believe.

Welsh   Like an alcoholic you paint me as half the time.

Coleman   Well, that isn't a big job of painting. A bent child with no paint could paint you as an alcoholic. There's no great effort needed in that.

Welsh   I never touched the stuff before I came to this parish. This parish would drive you to drink.

Coleman   I suppose it would, only some people don't need as much of a drive as others. Some need only a short walk.

Welsh   I'm no alcoholic, Coleman. I like a drink is all.

Coleman   Oh aye, and I believe you too. (*Pause.*) Vol-au-vents, feck. The white-haired oul ghoulish fecking whore. She's owed me the price of a pint since nineteen-seventy-fecking-seven. It's always tomorrow with that bitch. I don't care if she does have Alzheimer's. If I had a vol-au-vent I'd shove it up her arse.

Welsh   That's not a nice thing to be saying about a –

Coleman   I don't care if it is or it isn't.

Welsh (*pause*)   This house, isn't it going to be awful lonesome now with yere dad gone?

Coleman   No.

Welsh   Ah it'll be a biteen lonesome I'm sure.

Coleman   If you're saying it'll be a biteen lonesome maybe it *will* be a biteen lonesome. I'll believe it if you're forcing it down me throat and sure aren't you the world's authority on lonesome?

Welsh   Are there no lasses on the horizon for ye, now ye're free and easy? Oh I'll bet there's hundreds.

Coleman   Only your mammy.

Welsh   It's a beautiful mood today you're in. (*Pause.*) Were you never in love with a girl, so, Coleman?

Coleman   I was in love with a girl one time, aye, not that it's any of your fecking business. At tech this was. Alison O'Hoolihan. This gorgeous red hair on her. But she got a pencil stuck in the back of her gob one day. She was sucking it the pointy-end inwards. She must've gotten a nudge. That was the end of me and Alison O'Hoolihan.

Welsh   Did she die, Coleman?

Coleman   She didn't die, no. I wish she had, the bitch. No, she got engaged to the bastarding doctor who wrenched the pencil out for her. Anybody could've done that job. It didn't need a doctor. I have no luck.

Pause. **Welsh** *drinks some more.* **Valene** *enters with a carrier bag, out of which he takes some new figurines and arranges them on the shelf.* **Coleman** *watches.*

Valene   Fibreglass.

Coleman (*pause*)   Feck fibreglass.

Valene   No, feck you instead of feck fibreglass.

Coleman   No, feck you two times instead of feck fibreglass ...

Welsh   Hey now!! (*Pause.*) Jesus!

Valene   He started it.

Welsh (*pause*)   Tom Hanlon I see he's back. I was speaking to him at the funeral. Did Tom know yere dad?

Coleman   Slightly he knew Dad. He arrested him five or six times for screaming at nuns.

Welsh   I remember hearing tell of that. That was an odd crime.

Coleman   Not that odd.

Welsh   Ah come on, now, it is.

Coleman   Oh if you say it is, Walsh, I suppose it is.

Valene   I do hate them fecking Hanlons.

Welsh   Why now, Val?

Valene   Why, is it? Didn't their Mairtin hack the ears off of poor Lassie, let him fecking bleed to death?

Coleman   You've no evidence at all it was Mairtin hacked the ears off of Lassie.

Valene   Didn't he go bragging about it to Blind Billy Pender?

Coleman   That's only hearsay evidence. You wouldn't get that evidence to stand up in a court of law. Not from a blind boy anyways.

Valene   I'd expect you to be agin me. Full well I'd expect it.

Coleman   That dog did nothing but bark anyways.

Valene   Well, barking doesn't deserve ears chopped off, Coleman. That's what dogs are supposed to do is bark, if you didn't know.

Coleman   Not at that rate of barking. They're meant to ease up now and then. That dog was going for the world's fecking barking record.

Welsh   And there's plenty enough hate in the world as it is, Valene Connor, without you adding to it over a dead dog.

Valene   Nobody'll notice a biteen more hate, so, if there's plenty enough hate in the world.

Welsh   A nice attitude that is for a –

Valene   Feck off and sling your sermons at Maureen Folan and Mick Dowd, so, if it's nice attitudes you're after, Walsh. Wouldn't that be more in your fecking line?

Welsh *bows his head and pours himself another drink.*

Coleman   That shut the fecker up.

Valene   It did. You see how quick he is to . . . That's my fecking poteen now! What's the . . . eh?

Coleman   He did come in pegging orders for a drink, now. What was I supposed to say to him, him just sticking Dad in the ground for us?

Valene   Your own you could've given him so.

Coleman   And wasn't I about to 'til I up and discovered me cupboard was bare.

Valene   Bare again, was it?

Coleman   Bare as a bald fella's arse.

Valene   Never unbare are your cupboards.

Coleman   I suppose they're not now, but isn't that life?

Welsh   And there's no such word as unbare.

Valene *stares at* **Welsh** *sternly.*

Coleman (*laughing*)   He's right!

Valene   Picking me up on me vocabulary is it, Welsh?

Coleman   It is, aye.

Welsh   I'm not now. I'm only codding ya, Val.

Valene   And shaking the hands of Mick and Maureen weren't you, too, I saw you at the grave there, and passing chit-chat among ye . . .

Welsh   I was passing no chit-chat . . .

Valene   A great parish it is you run, one of them murdered his missus, an axe through her head, the other her mammy, a poker took her brains out, and it's only chit-chatting it is you be with them? Oh aye.

Welsh   What can I do, sure, if the courts and the polis . . .

Valene   Courts and the polis me arse. I heard the fella you represent was of a higher authority than the courts and the fecking polis.

Welsh (*sadly*)   I heard the same thing, sure. I must've heard wrong. It seems like God has no jurisdiction in this town. No jurisdiction at all.

Valene *takes his bottle, mumbling, and pours himself a drink. Pause.*

Coleman   That's a great word, I think.

Valene   What word?

Coleman   Jurisdiction. I like J-words.

Valene   Jurisdiction's too Yankee-sounding for me. They never stop saying it on *Hill Street Blues.*

Coleman   It's better than unbare anyways.

Valene   Don't you be starting with me again, ya feck.

Coleman   I will do what I wish, Mr Figurine-man.

Valene   Leave me figurines out of it.

Coleman   How many more do ya fecking need?

Valene   Lots more! No, lots and lots more!

Coleman   Oh aye.

Valene   And where's me felt-tip pen, too, so I'll be giving them me 'V'?

Coleman   I don't know where your fecking felt-tip pen is.

Valene   Well, you had it doing beards in me *Woman's Own* yesterday!

Coleman   Aye, and you wrenched it from me near tore me hand off.

Valene   Is all you deserved . . .

Coleman   You probably went hiding it then.

On these words, **Valene** *instantly remembers where his pen is and exits to his room. Pause.*

Coleman   He's forever hiding things that fella.

Welsh   I'm a terrible priest, so I am. I can never be defending God when people go saying things agin him, and, sure, isn't that the main qualification for being a priest?

Coleman   Ah there be a lot worse priests than you, Father, I'm sure. The only thing with you is you're a bit too weedy and you're a terror for the drink and you have doubts about Catholicism. Apart from that you're a fine priest. Number one you don't go abusing five-year-olds, so, sure, doesn't that give you a head start over half the priests in Ireland?

Welsh   That's no comfort at all, and them figures are over-exaggerated anyways. I'm a terrible priest, and I run a terrible parish, and that's the end of the matter. Two murderers I have on me books, and I can't get either of the beggars to confess to it. About betting on the horses and impure thoughts is all them bastards ever confess.

Coleman   Em, only I don't think you should be telling me what people be confessing, Father. You can be excommunicated for that I think. I saw it in a film with Montgomery Clift.

Welsh   Do ya see? I'm shite sure.

Coleman   Too hard on yourself is all you are, and it's only pure gossip that Mick and Maureen murdered anybody, and nothing but gossip. Mick's missus was a pure drink-driving accident is unfortunate but could've happened to anybody . . .

Welsh   With the scythe hanging out of her forehead, now, Coleman?

Coleman   A pure drink-driving, and Maureen's mam only fell down a big hill and Maureen's mam was never steady on her feet.

Welsh   And was even less steady with the brains pouring out of her, a poker swipe.

Coleman   She had a bad hip and everybody knew, and if it's at anybody you should be pegging murder accusations, isn't it me? Shot me dad's head off him, point-blank range.

Welsh   Aye, but an accident that was, and you had a witness . . .

Coleman   Is what I'm saying. And if Valene hadn't happened to be there to see me tripping and the gun falling, wouldn't the town be saying I put the barrel bang up agin him, blew the head off him on purpose? It's only because poor Mick and Maureen had no witnesses is why all them gobshites do go gossiping about them.

Valene *returns with his pen and starts drawing 'V's on the new figurines.*

Welsh   See? You do see the good in people, Coleman. That's what I'm supposed to do, but I don't. I'm always at the head of the queue to be pegging the first stone.

Valene   He's not having another fecking crisis of faith?

Coleman   He is.

Valene   He never stops, this fella.

Welsh   Aye, because I have nothing to offer me parish at all.

Coleman   Sure haven't you just coached the under-twelves football to the Connaught semi-finals yere first year trying?

Welsh   Ah the under-twelves football isn't enough to restore your faith in the priesthood, Coleman, and we're a bunch of foulers anyway.

Coleman   Ye aren't. Ye're skilful.

Welsh   Ten red cards in four games, Coleman. That's a world's record in girls' football. That'd be a record in boys' football. One of the lasses from St Angela's she's still in hospital after meeting us.

Coleman   If she wasn't up for the job she shouldn't've been on the field of play.

Welsh   Them poor lasses used to go off crying. Oh a great coach I am, oh aye.

Coleman   Sissy whining bitches is all them little feckers are.

A rap on the front door, then **Girleen**, *a pretty girl of seventeen, puts her head round it.*

Girleen   Are ye in need?

Valene   Come in for yourself, Girleen. I'll be taking a couple of bottles off ya, aye. I'll get me money.

He exits to his room as **Girleen** *enters, taking two bottles of poteen out of her bag.*

Girleen   Coleman. Father Welsh Walsh Welsh . . .

Welsh   Welsh.

Girleen   Welsh. I know. Don't be picking me up. How is all?

Coleman   We've just stuck our dad in the ground.

Girleen   Grand, grand. I met the postman on the road with a letter for Valene.

She lays an official-looking envelope on table.

That postman fancies me, d'you know? I think he'd like to be getting into me knickers, in fact I'm sure of it.

Coleman   Him and the rest of Galway, Girleen.

Welsh *puts his head in his hands at this talk.*

Girleen   Galway minimum. The EC more like. Well, a fella won't be getting into my knickers on a postman's wages. I'll tell you that, now.

Coleman Are you charging for entry so, Girleen?

Girleen I'm tinkering with the idea, Coleman. Why, are you interested? It'll take more than a pint and a bag of Taytos, mind.

Coleman I have a three-pound postal order somewhere I never used.

Girleen That's nearer the mark, now. (*To* **Welsh**.) What kind of wages do priests be on, Father?

Welsh Will you stop now?! Will you stop?! Isn't it enough for a girl going round flogging poteen, not to go talking of whoring herself on top of it?!

Girleen Ah, we're only codding you, Father.

She fluffs her fingers through **Welsh**'s *hair. He brushes her off.*

Girleen (*to* **Coleman**) He's not having another crisis of faith is he? That's twelve this week. We should report him to Jesus.

Welsh *moans into his hands.* **Girleen** *giggles slightly.* **Valene** *enters and pays* **Girleen**.

Valene Two bottles, Girleen.

Girleen Two bottles it is. You've a letter there.

Coleman Buy me a bottle, Valene. I'll owe ya.

Valene (*opening letter*) Buy you a bottle me arse.

Coleman Do ya see this fella?

Girleen You've diddled me out of a pound, Valene.

Valene *pays up as if expecting it.*

Valene It was worth a go.

Girleen You're the king of stink-scum fecking filth-bastards you, ya bitch-feck, Valene.

Welsh Don't be swearing like that now, Girleen . . .

Girleen Ah me hairy arse, Father.

Valene (*re letter*) Yes! It's here! It's here! Me cheque! And look how much too!

Valene *holds the cheque up in front of* **Coleman**'s *face.*

Coleman   I see how much.

Valene   Do ya see?

Coleman   I see now, and out of me face take it.

Valene (*holding it closer*)   Do ya see how much, now?

Coleman   I see now.

Valene   And all to me. Is it a closer look you do need?

Coleman   Out of me face take that thing now.

Valene   But maybe it's closer you need to be looking now . . .

Valene *rubs the cheque in* **Coleman**'s *face.* **Coleman** *jumps up and grabs* **Valene** *by the neck.* **Valene** *grabs him in the same way.* **Girleen** *laughs as they struggle together.* **Welsh** *darts drunkenly across and breaks the two apart.*

Welsh   Be stopping, now! What's the matter with ye?

Welsh *gets accidentally kicked as the brothers part. He winces.*

Coleman   I'm sorry, Father. I was aiming at that feck.

Welsh   Hurt that did! Bang on me fecking shin.

Girleen   You'll know now how the lasses at St Angela's be feeling.

Welsh   What's the matter with ye at all, sure?

Valene   He started it.

Welsh   Two brothers laying into each other the same day their father was buried! I've never heard the like.

Girleen   It's all because you're such a terrible priest to them, Father.

Welsh *glares at her. She looks away, smiling.*

Girleen   I'm only codding you, Father.

Welsh   What kind of a town is this at all? Brothers fighting and lasses peddling booze and two fecking murderers on the loose?

Girleen   And me pregnant on top of it. (*Pause.*) I'm not really.

Welsh *looks at her and them sadly, moving somewhat drunkenly to the door.*

Welsh   Don't be fighting any more, now, ye's two. (*Exits.*)

Girleen   Father Walsh Welsh has no sense of humour. I'll walk him the road home for himself, and see he doesn't get hit be a cow like the last time.

Coleman   See you so, Girleen.

Valene   See you so, Girleen. (**Girleen** *exits. Pause.*) That fella, eh?

Coleman (*in agreement*)   Eh? That fella.

Valene   Jeez. Eh? If he found out you blew the head off Dad on purpose, he'd probably get three times as maudlin.

Coleman   He takes things too much to heart does that fella.

Valene   Way too much to heart.

Blackout.

Scene Two

Evening. Against the back wall and blocking out the fireplace is now situated a large, new, orange stove with a big 'V' scrawled on its front. **Coleman**, *in glasses, sits in the armchair left, reading* Woman's Own, *a glass of poteen beside him.* **Valene** *enters, carrying a bag. Slowly, deliberately, he places a hand on the stove in a number of places in case it's been used recently.* **Coleman** *snorts in disgust at him.*

Valene   I'm checking.

Coleman   I can see you're checking.

Valene   I like to have a little check with you around.

Coleman   That's what you do best is check.

Valene   Just a biteen of a check, like. D'you know what I mean? In *my* opinion, like.

Coleman   I wouldn't touch your stove if you shoved a kettle up me arse.

Valene   Is right, my stove.

Coleman   If you fecking paid me I wouldn't touch your stove.

Valene   Well, I won't be fecking paying you to touch me stove.

Coleman   I know well you won't, you tight-fisted feck.

Valene   And *my* stove is right. Did *you* pay the three hundred? Did *you* get the gas fixed up? No. Who did? Me. My money. Was it your money? No, it was my money.

Coleman   I know well it was your money.

Valene   If you'd made a contribution I'd've said go ahead and use me stove, but you didn't, so I won't.

Coleman   We don't even need a stove.

Valene   You may not need a stove, but I need a stove.

Coleman   You never fecking eat, sure!

Valene   I'll start! Aye, by Christ I'll start. (*Pause.*) This stove is mine, them figurines are mine, this gun, them chairs, that table's mine. What else? This floor, them cupboards, everything in this fecking house is mine, and you don't go touching, boy. Not without me express permission.

Coleman   It'll be hard not to touch your fecking floor, now.

Valene   Not without me express . . .

Coleman   Unless I go fecking levitating.

Valene   Not without me express . . .

Coleman   Like them darkies.

Valene (*angrily*)   Not without me express fecking permission I'm saying!

Coleman   Your express permission, oh aye.

Valene   To *me* all this was left. To me and me alone.

Coleman   'Twasn't left but 'twas *awarded*.

Valene   Me and me alone.

Coleman   Awarded it was.

Valene   And you don't go touching. (*Pause.*) What darkies?

Coleman   Eh?

Valene   What darkies go levitating?

Coleman   Them darkies. On them carpets. Them levitating darkies.

Valene   Them's Pakis. Not darkies at all!

Coleman   The same differ!

Valene   Not at all the same differ! Them's Paki-men, same as whistle at the snakes.

Coleman   It seems like you're the expert on Paki-men!

Valene   I *am* the expert on Paki-men!

Coleman   You probably go falling in love with Paki-men too, so! Oh I'm sure.

Valene   Leave falling in love out of it.

Coleman   What did you get shopping, Mister 'I-want-to-marry-a-Paki-man'?

Valene   What did I get shopping, is it?

He takes two figurines out of his bag and arranges them delicately on the shelf.

Coleman   Ah for feck's sake . . .

Valene   Don't be cursing now. Coleman. Not in front of the saints. Against God that is.

He takes eight packets of Taytos out of the bag and lays them on the table.

And some Taytos I got.

Coleman   Be getting McCoys if you're getting crisps.

Valene   I'll be getting what I li—

Coleman   Ya fecking cheapskate.

Valene (*pause. Glaring*)   I'm not getting some crisps taste exactly the same, cost double, Coleman.

Coleman   They don't taste the same and they have grooves.

Valene   They do taste the same and feck grooves.

Coleman   Taytos are dried fecking filth and everybody knows they are.

Valene   The crisp expert now I'm listening to. What matter if they're dried fecking filth? They're seventeen pee, and whose crisps are they anyways? They're my crisps.

Coleman   They're your crisps.

Valene   My crisps and my crisps alone.

Coleman   Or get Ripples.

Valene   Ripples me arse and I don't see you digging in your . . . what's this?

He picks up **Coleman**'s *glass and sniffs it.*

Coleman   What's wha?

Valene   This.

Coleman   Me own.

Valene   Your own your arse. You've no money to be getting your own.

Coleman   I do have.

Valene   From where?

Coleman   Am I being interrogated now?

Valene   You are.

Coleman   Feck ya so.

Valene *takes his poteen out of his biscuit tin to check if any is missing.*
Coleman *puts the magazine aside, takes his glasses off and sits at the table.*

Valene   You've been at this.

Coleman   I haven't at all been at that.

Valene   It seems very . . . reduced.

Coleman   Reduced me arse. I wouldn't be at yours if you shoved a fecking . . .

Valene (*sipping it, uncertain*)   You've topped it up with water.

Coleman   Be believing what you wish. I never touched your poteen.

Valene   Where would you get money for . . . Me house insurance?! Oh you fecker . . . !

He desperately finds and examines his insurance book.

Coleman   I paid in your house insurance.

Valene   This isn't Duffy's signature.

Coleman   It is Duffy's signature. Doesn't it say 'Duffy'?

Valene   You paid it?

Coleman   Aye.

Valene   Why?

Coleman   Oh to do you a favour, after all the favours you've done me over the years. Oh aye.

Valene   It's easy enough to check.

Coleman   It *is* easy enough to check, and check ahead, ya feck. Check until you're blue in the face.

Confused, **Valene** *puts the book away.*

Coleman   It's not only money can buy you booze. No. Sex appeal it is too.

Valene   Sex appeal? You? Your sex appeal wouldn't buy the phlegm off a dead frog.

Coleman   You have your own opinion and you're well entitled to it. Girleen's of the opposite opinion.

Valene   Girleen? Me arse.

Coleman   Is true.

Valene   Eh?

Coleman   I said let me have a bottle on tick and I'll be giving you a big kiss, now. She said, 'If you let me be touching you below, sure you can have a bottle for nothing.' The deal was struck then and there.

Valene   Girleen wouldn't touch you below if you bought her a pony, let alone giving poteen away on top of it.

Coleman   I can only be telling the God's honest truth, and how else would I be getting poteen for free?

Valene (*unsure*)   Me arse. (*Pause.*) Eh? (*Pause.*) Girleen's pretty. (*Pause.*) Girleen's awful pretty. (*Pause.*) Why would Girleen be touching you below?

Coleman   Mature men it is Girleen likes.

Valene   I don't believe you at all.

Coleman   Don't so.

Valene (*pause*)   What did it feel like?

Coleman   What did what feel like?

Valene   The touching below.

Coleman   Em, nice enough now.

Valene (*unsure*)   I don't believe you at all. (*Pause.*) No, I don't believe you at all.

Coleman *opens and starts eating a packet of* **Valene**'s *crisps.*

Valene   Girleen wouldn't be touching you below. Never in the world would Girleen be touching y— (*Stunned.*) Who said you could go eating me crisps?!

Coleman   Nobody said.

Valene   In front of me?!

Coleman   I decided of me own accord.

Valene   You'll be paying me seventeen pee of your own accord so! And right now you'll be paying me!

Coleman   Right now, is it?

Valene   It is!

Coleman   The money you have stashed?

Valene   And if you don't pay up it's a batter I'll be giving you.

Coleman   A batter from you? I'd be as scared of a batter from a lemon.

Valene   Seventeen pee I'm saying!

Pause. **Coleman** *slowly takes a coin out of his pocket and, without looking at it, slams it down on the table.*

Valene (*looks at the coin*)   That's ten.

Coleman *looks at the coin, takes out another one and slams that down also.*

Coleman   You can keep the change.

Valene   I can keep the change, can I?

He pockets the coins, takes out three pee, opens one of **Coleman***'s hands and places the money in it.*

Valene   I'm in no need of charity.

He turns away. Still sitting, **Coleman** *throws the coins hard at the back of* **Valene***'s head.*

Valene   Ya fecker ya!! Come on so!

Coleman *jumps up, knocking his chair over.*

Coleman   Come on so, is it?

Valene   Pegging good money at me?!

Coleman   It is. And be picking that money up now, for your oul piggy-bank, ya little virgin fecking gayboy ya . . .

The two grapple, fall to the floor and roll around scuffling. **Welsh** *enters through the front door, slightly drunk.*

Welsh   Hey ye's two! Ye's two! (*Pause. Loudly.*) Ye's two!

Coleman (*irritated*)   Wha?

Welsh   Tom Hanlon's just killed himself.

Valene   Eh?

Welsh   Tom Hanlon's just killed himself.

Valene (*pause*)   Let go o' me neck, you.

Coleman   Let go o' me arm so.

The two slowly let go of each other and stand up, as **Welsh** *sits at the table, stunned.*

Welsh   He walked out into the lake from the oul jetty there. Aye, and kept walking. His body's on the shingle. His father had to haul me drunk out of Rory's to say a prayer o'er him, and me staggering.

Valene   Tom Hanlon? Jeez. Sure I was only talking to Tom a day ago there. The funeral.

Welsh   A child seen him. Seen him sitting on the bench on the jetty, a pint with him, looking out across the lake to the mountains there. And when his pint was done he got up and started walking, the clothes still on him, and didn't stop walking. No. 'Til the poor head of him was under. And even then he didn't stop.

Coleman (*pause*)   Ah I never liked that Tom fecking Hanlon. He was always full of himself, same as all fecking coppers . . .

Welsh (*angrily*)   The poor man's not even cold yet, Coleman Connor. Do you have to be talking that way about him?

Coleman   I do, or if I'm not to be a hypocrite anyways I do.

Valene   It's hypocrites now. Do you see this fella, Father? Ate a bag of me crisps just now without a by your leave . . .

Coleman   I paid you for them crisps . . .

Valene   Then says he's not a hypocrite.

Coleman   I paid thruppence over the odds for them crisps, and how does eating crisps make you a hypocrite anyways?

Valene   It just does. And interfering with a schoolgirl on top of it is another crime, Father.

Coleman   I interfered with no schoolgirl. I was interfered with *be* a schoolgirl.

Valene   The same differ!

Welsh   What schoolgirl's this, now?

Coleman   Girleen this schoolgirl is. This afternoon there she came up and a fine oul time we had, oh aye.

Welsh   Girleen? Sure Girleen's been helping me wash the strips for the under-twelves football all day, never left me sight.

Embarrassed, **Coleman** *gets up and moves towards his room.* **Valene** *blocks his way.*

Valene   Aha! Aha! Now who's the virgin fecking gayboy, eh? Now who's the virgin fecking gayboy?

Coleman   Out of me way, now.

Valene   *Now*, eh?

Coleman   Out of me way I'm saying.

Valene   I knew well!

Coleman   Are you moving or am I moving ya?

Valene *Now* did I know well? Eh?

Coleman Eh?

Valene Eh?

Welsh Coleman, come back now. We –

Coleman And you can shut your fecking gob too, Welsh or Walsh or whatever your fecking name is, ya priest! You don't go catching Coleman Connor out on lies and expect to be . . . and be expecting to . . . to be . . .

He enters his room, slamming its door.

Valene You're a stuttering oul ass, so you are! 'To be . . . to be . . . to be . . . ' (*To* **Welsh.**) Eh?

As **Valene** *turns back to* **Welsh,** **Coleman** *dashes out, kicks the stove and dashes back to his room,* **Valene** *trying and failing to catch him.*

Valene Ya fecker, ya!

He checks the stove for damage.

Me good fecking stove! If there's any damage done to this stove it'll be you'll be paying for it, ya feck! Did you see that, Father? Isn't that man mad? (*Pause.*) Do ya like me new stove, Father? Isn't it a good one?

Coleman (*off*) Do ya see that 'V' on his stove, Father? Do you think it's a V for Valene? It isn't. It's a V for Virgin, it is.

Valene Oh is it now . . . ?

Coleman (*off*) V for Virgin it is, uh-huh.

Valene When you're the king of the virgins?

Coleman (*off*) Valene the Virgin that V stands for.

Valene The fecking king of them you are! And don't be listening at doors!

Coleman (*off*) I'll be doing what I wish.

Valene *checks stove again.* **Welsh** *is on the verge of tears.*

Valene (*re stove*) No, I think it's okay, now . . .

Welsh   You see, I come in to ye . . . and ye're fighting. Fair enough, now, that's all ye two ever do is fight. Ye'll never be changed. It's enough times I've tried . . .

Valene   Are you crying, Father, or is it a bit of a cold you do have? Ah it's a cold . . .

Welsh   It's crying I am.

Valene   Well, I've never seen the like.

Welsh   Cos I come in, and I tell ya a fella's just gone and killed himself, a fella ye went to school with . . . a fella ye grew up with . . . a fella never had a bad word to say about anybody and did his best to be serving the community every day of his life . . . and I tell you he's killed himself be drowning, is a horrible way to die, and not only do ye not bat an eye . . . not only do ye not bat an eye but ye go arguing about crisps and stoves then!

Valene   I batted an eye.

Welsh   I didn't notice that eye batted!

Valene   I batted a big eye.

Welsh   Well, I didn't notice it, now!

Valene (*pause*)   But isn't it a nice stove, Father?

Welsh *puts his head in his hands.*

Valene *goes to the stove.*

Valene   Only a day I've had it fixed up. You can still smell as clean as it is. Coleman's forbid to touch it at all because Coleman didn't contribute a penny towards it, for Coleman doesn't *have* a penny to contribute towards it. (*Picks up the three pee.*) He has three pee, but three pee won't go too far towards a stove. Not too far at all. He threw this three pee at me head earlier, d'you know? (*In realisation, angrily.*) And if he has no money and he wasn't interfered with, where the feck was it that poteen did come from?! Coleman . . . !

Welsh (*screamed*)   Valene, you fecking fecker ya!!

Valene   Wha? Oh, aye, poor Thomas.

He nods in phoney empathy.

Welsh (*pause. Sadly, standing*)   I came up to get ye to come to the lake with me, to be dragging poor Tom's body home for himself. Will ye be helping now?

Valene   I will be, Father. I will be.

Welsh (*pause*)   Feck. Two murders and a suicide now. Two murders and a fecking suicide . . .

He exits, shaking his head.

Valene (*calling out*)   Sure, not your fault was it, Father. Don't you be getting maudlin again! (*Pause.*) Coleman? I'm off down −

Coleman (*off*)   I heard.

Valene   Are ya coming so?

Coleman (*off*)   Not at all am I coming. To go humping a dead policeman about the country? A dead policeman used to laugh at me press-ups in PE? I don't fecking think so, now.

Valene   You forever bear a grudge, you. Ah anyways it's good strong men Father Walsh does need helping him, not virgin fecking gayboys couldn't pay a drunk monkey to go interfering with him.

He quickly exits. **Coleman** *storms into the room to find him gone. He goes to the door and idles there, thinking, looking around the room. His gaze falls on the stove. He picks up some matches and opens the stove door.*

Coleman   A virgin fecking gayboy, is it? Shall we be having gas mark ten for no reason at all, now? We shall, d'you know?

He lights the stove, turns it up, closes its door and exits to his room. He returns a few seconds later and looks around the room.

For no reason at all, is it?

He takes a large oven-proof bowl out of a cupboard, places all of the figurines from the shelf into the bowl and puts the bowl inside the stove, closing its door afterwards.

Now we'll be seeing who's a virgin gayboy couldn't pay a monkey to interfere with him. I'll say we'll fecking see.

He pulls on his jacket, brushes his unkempt hair for two seconds with a manky comb, and exits through the front door. Blackout.

Scene Three

A few hours later. **Valene** *and* **Welsh** *enter, slightly drunk.* **Valene** *takes his poteen out of his tin and pours himself a glass.* **Welsh** *eyes it a little.*

Valene   That was an awful business, eh?

Welsh   Terrible. Just terrible, now. And I couldn't say a thing to them. Not a thing.

Valene   What could be said to them, sure? The only thing they wanted to hear was 'Your son isn't dead at all', and that wouldn't have worked. Not with him lying in their front room, dripping.

Welsh   Did you ever hear such crying, Valene?

Valene   You could've filled a lake with the tears that family cried. Or a russaway at minimum.

Welsh (*pause*)   A wha?

Valene   A russaway. One of them russaways.

Welsh   Reservoir?

Valene   Russaway, aye, and their Mairtin crying with the best of them. I've never seen Mairtin crying as hard. I suppose that's all you deserve for chopping the ears off a poor dog.

Welsh   I suppose if it's your only brother you lose you do cry hard.

Valene   I wouldn't cry hard if I lost me only brother. I'd buy a big cake and have a crowd round.

Welsh   Ah Valene, now. If it's your own brother you can't get on with, how can we ever hope for peace in the world . . . ?

Valene   Peace me arse and don't keep going on, you. You always do whine on this oul subject when you're drunk.

He sits at the table with drink and bottle.

Welsh (*pause*)   A lonesome oul lake that is for a fella to go killing himself in. It makes me sad just to think of it. To think of poor Tom sitting alone there, alone with his thoughts, the cold lake in front of him, and him weighing up what's best, a life full of the loneliness that took him there but a life full of good points too. Every life has good points, even if it's only . . . seeing rivers, or going travelling, or watching football on the telly . . .

Valene (*nodding*)   Football, aye . . .

Welsh   Or the hopes of being loved. And Thomas weighing all that up on the one hand, then weighing up a death in cold water on the other, and choosing the water. And first it strikes you as dumb, and a waste, 'You were thirty-eight years old, you had health and friends, there was plenty worse-off fecks than you in the world, Tom Hanlon' . . .

Valene   The girl born with no lips in Norway.

Welsh   I didn't hear about her.

Valene   There was this girl in Norway, and she was born with no lips at all.

Welsh   Uh-huh. But then you say if the world's such a decent place worth staying in, where were his friends when he needed them in this decent world? When he needed them most, to say, 'Come away from there, ya daft, we'd miss ya, you're worthwhile, as dumb as you are.' Where were his friends then? Where was I then? Sitting pissed on me own in a pub. (*Pause.*) Rotting in hell now, Tom Hanlon is. According to the Catholic Church anyways he is, the same as every suicide. No remorse. No mercy on him.

Valene   Is that right now? Every suicide you're saying?

Welsh   According to us mob it's right anyways.

Valene   Well, I didn't know that. That's a turn-up for the books. (*Pause.*) So the fella from *Alias Smith and Jones,* he'd be in hell?

Welsh   I don't know the fella from *Alias Smith and Jones.*

Valene   Not the blond one, now, the other one.

Welsh   I don't know the fella.

Valene   He killed himself, and at the height of his fame.

Welsh   Well, if he killed himself, aye, he'll be in hell too. (*Pause.*) It's great it is. You can kill a dozen fellas, you can kill two dozen fellas. So long as you're sorry after you can still get into heaven. But if it's yourself you go murdering, no. Straight to hell.

Valene   That sounds awful harsh. (*Pause.*) So Tom'll be in hell now, he will? Jeez. (*Pause.*) I wonder if he's met the fella from *Alias Smith and Jones* yet? Ah, that fella must be old be now. Tom probably wouldn't even recognise him. That's if he saw *Alias Smith and Jones* at all. I only saw it in England. It mightn't've been on telly here at all.

Welsh (*sighing*)   You wouldn't be sparing a drop of that poteen would ya, Valene? I've an awful thirst . . .

Valene   Ah, Father, I have only a drop left and I need that for meself . . .

Welsh   You've half the bottle, sure . . .

Valene   And if I had some I'd spare it, but I don't, and should priests be going drinking anyways? No they shouldn't, or anyways not on the night . . .

Welsh   Thou shouldst share and share alike the Bible says. Or somewhere it says . . .

Valene   Not on the night you let one of your poor flock go murdering himself you shouldn't, is what me sentence was going to be.

Welsh   Well, was that a nice thing to be saying?! Do I need that, now?!

Valene (*mumbling*)   Don't go trying to go cadging a poor fella's drink off him so, the wages you're on.

He gets up, puts the bottle back in his biscuit tin and carefully Sellotapes the lid up, humming as he does so.

Welsh   Is there a funny smell off of your house tonight, Val, now?

Valene   If you're going criticising the smell of me house you can be off now, so you can.

Welsh   Like of plastic, now?

Valene   Cadging me booze and then saying me house smells. That's the best yet, that is.

Welsh (*pause*)   At least Coleman came down to help us with poor Thomas after all, even if he was late. But that was awful wrong of him to go asking Tom's poor mam if she'd be doing vol-au-vents after.

Valene   That was awful near the mark.

Welsh   And her sitting there crying, and him nudging her then, and again and again, 'Will ye be having vol-au-vents, Missus, will ye?'

Valene   If he was drunk you could excuse it, but he wasn't. It was just out of spite. (*Laughing.*) Although it was funny, now.

Welsh   Where is he anyways? I thought he was walking the road with us.

Valene   He'd stopped to do up his shoelaces a way back. (*Pause. In realisation.*) Coleman *has* no shoelaces. He has only loafers. (*Pause.*) Where have all me Virgin Marys gone?!

He leans in over the stove, placing his hands on its top, to see if the figurines have fallen down the back. The searing heat from the stove burns his hands and he pulls them away, yelping.

(*Hysterical.*) Wha?! Wha?!

Welsh   What is it, Valene? Did you go leaving your stove on?

Stunned, **Valene** *opens the stove door with a towel. Smoke billows out. He takes the steaming bowl of molten plastic out, sickened, places it on the table and delicately picks up one of the half-melted figurines with the towel.*

Welsh   All your figurines are melted, Valene.

Valene (*staggering backwards*)   I'll kill the feck! I'll kill the feck!

Welsh   I'll be betting it was Coleman, Valene.

Valene   That's all there is to it! I'll kill the feck!

Valene *pulls the shotgun off the wall and marches around the room in a daze, as* **Welsh** *jumps up and tries to calm him.*

Welsh   Oh Valene now! Put that gun down!

Valene   I'll blow the head off him! The fecking head off him I'll blow! I tell him not to touch me stove and I tell him not to touch me figurines and what does he do? He cooks me figurines in me stove! (*Looking into bowl.*) That one was blessed be the Pope! That one was given me mammy be Yanks! And they're all gone! All of them! They're all just the fecking heads and bobbing around!

Welsh   You can't go shooting your brother o'er inanimate objects, Valene! Give me that gun, now.

Valene   Inanimate objects? Me figurines of the saints? And you call yoursel' a priest? No wonder you're the laughing stock of the Catholic Church in Ireland. And that takes some fecking doing, boy.

Welsh   Give it me now, I'm saying. Your own flesh and blood this is you're talking of murdering.

Valene   Me own flesh and blood is right, and why not? If he's allowed to murder his own flesh and blood and get away with it, why shouldn't I be?

Welsh What are you talking about, now? Coleman shooting your dad was a pure accident and you know well.

Valene A pure accident me arse! You're the only fecker in Leenane believes that shooting was an accident. Didn't Dad make a jibe about Coleman's hairstyle, and didn't Coleman dash out, pull him back be the hair and blow the poor skulleen out his head, the same as he'd been promising to do since the age of eight and Da trod on his Scalectrix, broke it in two . . .

Coleman *enters through the front door.*

Coleman Well, I did love that Scalectrix. It had glow-in-the-dark headlamps.

Valene *turns and points the gun at* **Coleman**. **Welsh** *backs off moaning, hands to his head.* **Coleman** *nonchalantly idles to the table and sits down.*

Welsh It can't be true! It can't be true!

Coleman Look at that fella gone pure white . . .

Valene No, shut up, you! Don't be coming in mouthing after your fecking crimes . . .

Welsh Tell me you didn't shoot your dad on purpose, Coleman. Please, now . . .

Valene This isn't about our fecking dad! This is about me fecking figurines!

Coleman Do you see this fella's priorities?

Valene Melting figurines is against God outright!

Welsh So is shooting your dad in the head, sure!

Valene And on gas mark ten!

Welsh Tell me, Coleman, tell me, please. Tell me you didn't shoot your dad there on purpose. Oh tell me, now . . .

Coleman Will you calm down, you? (*Pause.*) Of course I shot me dad on purpose.

Welsh *starts groaning again.*

Coleman I don't take criticising from nobody. 'Me hair's like a drunken child's.' I'd only just combed me hair and there was nothing wrong with it! And I know well shooting your dad in the head is against God, but there's some insults that can never be excused.

Valene And cooking figurines is against God on top of it, if they're Virgin Mary figurines anyways.

Coleman Is true enough, be the fella with the gun, and I'll tell you another thing that's against God, before this fella puts a bullet in me . . . (*To* **Welsh**.) Hey, moany, are you listening . . . ?

Welsh I'm listening, I'm listening, I'm listening . . .

Coleman I'll tell you another thing that's against God. Sitting your brother in a chair, with his dad's brains dripping down him, and promising to tell everyone it was nothing but an accident . . .

Valene Shut up now, ya feck . . .

Coleman So long as there and then you sign over everything your dad went and left you in his will . . .

Welsh No . . . no . . . no . . .

Coleman His house and his land and his tables and his chairs and his bit of money to go frittering away on shitey-arsed ovens you only got to torment me, ya feck . . .

Welsh No, now . . . no . . .

Valene Be saying goodbye to the world, you, fecker!

Coleman And fecking Taytos then, the worst crisps in the world . . .

Valene *cocks the gun that's up against* **Coleman***'s head.*

Welsh No, Valene, no!

Valene I said say goodbye to the world, ya feck.

Coleman Goodbye to the world, ya feck.

Valene *pulls the trigger. There is a hollow click. He pulls the trigger again. Another click. A third time, and another click, as* **Coleman** *reaches in his pocket and takes out two shotgun cartridges.*

Coleman   Do you think I'm fecking stupid, now? (*To* **Welsh**.) Did you see that, Father? My own brother going shooting me in the head.

Valene   Give me them fecking bullets, now.

Coleman   No.

Valene   Give me them bullets I'm saying.

Coleman   I won't.

Valene   Give me them fecking . . .

Valene *tries to wrench the bullets out of* **Coleman**'s *clenched fist,* **Coleman** *laughing as he does so.* **Valene** *grabs* **Coleman** *by the neck and they fall to the floor, grappling, rolling around the place.* **Welsh** *stares at the two of them dumbstruck, horrified. He catches sight of the bowl of steaming plastic beside him and, almost blankly, as the grappling continues, clenches his fists and slowly lowers them into the burning liquid, holding them under. Through clenched teeth and without breathing,* **Welsh** *manages to withhold his screaming for about ten or fifteen seconds until, still holding his fists under, he lets rip with a horrifying high-pitched wail lasting about ten seconds, during which* **Valene** *and* **Coleman** *stop fighting, stand, and try to help him . . .*

Valene   Father Walsh, now . . .

Coleman   Father Walsh, Father Walsh . . .

Welsh *pulls his fists out of the bowl, red raw, stifles his screams again, looks over the shocked* **Valene** *and* **Coleman** *in despair and torment, smashes the bowl off the table and dashes out through the front door, his fists clutched to his chest in pain.*

Welsh (*exiting, screaming*)   Me name's *Welsh*!!!

Valene *and* **Coleman** *stare after him a moment or two.*

Coleman   Sure that fella's pure mad.

Valene   He's outright mad.

Coleman   He's a lube. (*Gesturing at bowl.*) Will he be expecting us to clear his mess up?

Valene *puts his head out the front door and calls out.*

Valene   Will you be expecting us to clear your mess up, you?

Coleman (*pause*)   What did he say?

Valene   He was gone.

Coleman   A lube and nothing but a lube. (*Pause.*) Ah it's your fecking floor. You clean it up.

Valene   You wha?!

Coleman   Do you see me nice bullets, Valene?

Coleman *rattles his two bullets in* **Valene**'s *face, then exits to his room.*

Valene   Ya fecking . . . !

Coleman's *door slams shut.* **Valene** *grimaces, pauses, scratches his balls blankly and sniffs his fingers. Pause. Blackout.*

Interval.

Scene Four

A plain bench on a lakeside jetty at night, on which **Welsh** *sits with a pint, his hands lightly bandaged.* **Girleen** *comes over and sits down beside him.*

Welsh   Girleen.

Girleen   Father. What are ya up to?

Welsh   Just sitting here, now.

Girleen   Oh aye, aye. (*Pause.*) That was a nice sermon at Thomas's today, Father.

Welsh   I didn't see you there, did I?

Girleen   I was at the back a ways. (*Pause.*) Almost made me go crying, them words did.

Welsh You crying? I've never in all the years heard of you going crying, Girleen. Not at funerals, not at weddings. You didn't even cry when Holland knocked us out of the fecking World Cup.

Girleen Now and then on me now I go crying, over different things . . .

Welsh That Packie fecking Bonner. He couldn't save a shot from a fecking cow.

He sips his pint.

Girleen I'd be saying you've had a few now, Father?

Welsh Don't you be starting on me now. On top of everybody else.

Girleen I wasn't starting on ya.

Welsh Not today of all days.

Girleen I wasn't starting at all on ya. I do tease you sometimes but that's all I do do.

Welsh Sometimes, is it? All the time, more like, the same as everybody round here.

Girleen I do only tease you now and again, and only to camouflage the mad passion I have deep within me for ya . . .

Welsh *gives her a dirty look. She smiles.*

Girleen No, I'm only joking now, Father.

Welsh Do ya see?!

Girleen Ah be taking a joke will ya, Father? It's only cos you're so high-horse and up yourself that you make such an easy target.

Welsh I'm not so high-horse and up meself.

Girleen All right you're not so.

Welsh (*pause*) *Am* I so high-horse and up meself?

Girleen No, now. Well, no more than most priests.

Welsh   Maybe I am high-horse so. Maybe that's why I don't fit into this town. Although I'd have to have killed half me fecking relatives to fit into this town. Jeez. I thought Leenane was a nice place when first I turned up here, but no. Turns out it's the murder capital of fecking Europe. Did *you* know Coleman had killed his dad on purpose?

Girleen (*lowers head, embarrassed*)   I think I did hear a rumour somewhere along the line . . .

Welsh   A fecking rumour? And you didn't bat an eye or go reporting it?

Girleen   Sure I'm no fecking stool-pigeon and Coleman's dad was always a grumpy oul feck. He did kick me cat Eamonn there once.

Welsh   A fella deserves to die, so, for kicking a cat?

Girleen (*shrugs*)   It depends on the fella. And the cat. But there'd be a lot less cats kicked in Ireland, I'll tell ya, if the fella could rest assured he'd be shot in the head after.

Welsh   You have no morals at all, it seems, Girleen.

Girleen   I have plenty of morals only I don't keep whining on about them like some fellas.

Welsh (*pause*)   Val and Coleman'll kill each other someday if somebody doesn't do something to stop them. It won't be me who stops them anyways. It'll be someone with guts for the job.

He takes out a letter and passes it to **Girleen**.

Welsh   I've written them a little lettereen here, Girleen, would you give it to them next time you see them?

Girleen   Won't you be seeing them soon enough yourself?

Welsh   I won't be. I'm leaving Leenane tonight.

Girleen   Leaving for where?

Welsh   Anywhere. Wherever they send me. Anywhere but here.

Girleen   But why, Father?

Welsh   Ah lots of different reasons, now, but the three slaughterings and one suicide amongst me congregation didn't help.

Girleen   But none of that was your fault, Father.

Welsh   Oh no?

Girleen   And don't you have the under-twelves semi-final tomorrow morning to be coaching?

Welsh   Them bitches have never listened to me advice before. I don't see why they should go starting now. Nobody ever listens to my advice. Nobody ever listens to me at all.

Girleen   I listen to you.

Welsh (*sarcastic*)   Ar that's great comfort.

Girleen *bows her head, hurt.*

Welsh   And you don't listen to me either. How many times have I told you to stop flogging your dad's booze about town, and still you don't?

Girleen   Ah it's just till I save up a few bob, Father, I'm doing that flogging.

Welsh   A few bob for what? To go skittering it away the clubs in Carraroe, and drunk schoolboys pawing at ya.

Girleen   Not at all, Father. I do save it to buy a few nice things out me mam's Freeman's catalogue. They do have an array of . . .

Welsh   To go buying shite, aye. Well, I wish I did have as tough problems in my life as you do in yours, Girleen. It does sound like life's a constant torment for ya.

Girleen *stands up and wrenches* **Welsh***'s head back by the hair.*

Girleen   If anybody else went talking to me that sarcastic I'd punch them in the fecking eye for them, only if I punched you in the fecking eye you'd probably go crying like a fecking girl!

Welsh   I never asked you to come sitting beside me.

Girleen   Well, I didn't know there was a law against sitting beside ya, although I wish there fecking was one now.

She releases him and starts walking away.

Welsh   I'm sorry for being sarcastic to you, Girleen, about your mam's catalogue and whatnot. I am.

Girleen *stops, pauses, and idles back to the bench.*

Girleen   It's okay.

Welsh   It's only that I'm feeling a bit . . . I don't know . . .

Girleen (*sitting beside him*)   Maudlin.

Welsh   Maudlin. Maudlin is right.

Girleen   Maudlin and lonesome. The maudlin and lonesome Father Walsh. *Welsh.* (*Pause.*) I'm sorry, Father.

Welsh   Nobody ever remembers.

Girleen   It's just Walsh is so close to Welsh, Father.

Welsh   I know it is. I know it is.

Girleen   What's your first name, Father?

Welsh (*pause*)   Roderick.

Girleen *stifles laughter.* **Welsh** *smiles.*

Girleen   Roderick? (*Pause.*) Roderick's a horrible name, Father.

Welsh   I know, and thanks for saying so, Girleen, but you're just trying to boost me spirits now, aren't ya?

Girleen   I'm just being nice to ya now.

Welsh   What kind of a name's Girleen for a girl anyways? What's your proper first name?

Girleen (*cringing*)   Mary.

Welsh (*laughing*)   Mary? And you go laughing at Roderick then?

Girleen   Mary's the name of the mammy of Our Lord, did you ever hear tell of it?

Welsh I heard of it somewhere along the line.

Girleen It's the reason she never got anywhere for herself. Fecking Mary.

Welsh *You'll* be getting somewhere for yourself, Girleen.

Girleen D'ya think so, now?

Welsh As tough a get as you are? Going threatening to thump priests? Of course.

Girleen *brushes the hair out of* **Welsh***'s eyes.*

Girleen I wouldn't have gone thumping you, now, Father.

She gently slaps his cheek.

Maybe a decent slapeen, now.

Welsh *smiles and faces front.* **Girleen** *looks at him, then away, embarrassed.*

Welsh (*pause*) No, I just came out to have a think about Thomas before I go on me way. Say a little prayer for him.

Girleen It's tonight you're going?

Welsh It's tonight, aye. I said to meself I'll stay for Tom's funeral, then that'll be the end of it.

Girleen But that's awful quick. No one'll have a chance to wish you goodbye, Father.

Welsh Goodbye, aye, and good riddance to the back of me.

Girleen Not at all.

Welsh No?

Girleen No.

Pause. **Welsh** *nods, unconvinced, and drinks again.*

Girleen Will you write to me from where you're going and be giving me your new address, Father?

Welsh I'll try, Girleen, aye.

Girleen   Just so's we can say hello now and then, now.

Welsh   Aye, I'll try.

As he speaks, **Girleen** *manages to stifle tears without him noticing.*

Welsh   This is where he walked in from, d'you know? Poor Tom. Look at as cold and bleak as it is. Do you think it took courage or stupidity for him to walk in, Girleen?

Girleen   Courage.

Welsh   The same as that.

Girleen   And Guinness.

Welsh (*laughing*)   The same as that. (*Pause.*) Look at as sad and as quiet and still.

Girleen   It's more than Thomas has killed himself here down the years, d'you know, Father? Three other fellas walked in here, me mam was telling me.

Welsh   Is that right now?

Girleen   Years and years ago this is. Maybe even famine times.

Welsh   Drowned themselves?

Girleen   This is where they all come.

Welsh   We should be scared of their ghosts so but we're not scared. Why's that?

Girleen   You're not scared because you're pissed to the gills. I'm not scared because . . . I don't know why. One, because you're here, and two, because . . . I don't know. I don't be scared of cemeteries at night either. The opposite of that, I do *like* cemeteries at night.

Welsh   Why, now? Because you're a morbid oul tough?

Girleen (*embarrassed throughout*)   Not at all. I'm not a tough. It's because . . . even if you're sad or something, or lonely or something, you're still better off than them lost in the ground or in the lake, because . . . at least you've got the *chance* of being happy, and even if it's a real little chance, it's more than them dead ones have. And it's not that you're saying 'Hah, I'm better than ye', no, because in the long run it might end up that you have a worse life than ever they had and you'd've been better off as dead as them, there and then. But at least when you're still here there's the *possibility* of happiness, and it's like them dead ones know that, and they're happy for you to have it. They say 'Good luck to ya.' (*Quietly.*) Is the way I see it anyways.

Welsh You have a million thoughts going on at the back of them big brown eyes of yours.

Girleen I never knew you did ever notice me big brown eyes. Aren't they gorgeous, now?

Welsh You'll grow up to be a mighty fine woman one day, Girleen, God bless you.

He drinks again.

Girleen (*quietly, sadly*) One day, aye. (*Pause.*) I'll be carrying on the road home for meself now, Father. Will you be staying or will you be walking with me?

Welsh I'll be staying a biteen longer for meself, Girleen. I'll be saying that prayer for poor Thomas, now.

Girleen It's goodbye for a while so.

Welsh It is.

Girleen *kisses his cheek and they hug* **Girleen** *stands.*

Welsh You'll remember to be giving that letter to Valene and Coleman, now, Girleen?

Girleen I will. What's in it, Father? It does sound very mysterious. It wouldn't be packed full of condoms for them, would it?

Welsh It wouldn't at all, now!

Girleen Cos, you know, Valene and Coleman'd get no use out of them, unless they went using them on a hen.

Welsh Girleen, now . . .

Girleen And it'd need to be a blind hen.

Welsh   You do have a terrible mouth on ya.

Girleen   Aye, all the better to . . . no, I won't be finishing that sentence. Did you hear tell of Valene's new hobby, Father? He's been roaming the entirety of Connemara picking up new figurines of the saints for himself, but only ceramic and china ones won't go melting away on him. Thirty-seven of them at last count he has, and only to go tormenting poor Coleman.

Welsh   Them two, they're just odd.

Girleen   They *are* odd. They're the kings of odd. (*Pause.*) See you so, Father.

Welsh   See you so, Girleen. Or Mary, is it?

Girleen   If you let me know where you get to I'll write with how the under-twelves get on tomorrow. It may be in the *Tribune* anyways. Under 'Girl decapitated in football match'.

Welsh *nods, half smiles.* **Girleen** *idles away.*

Welsh   Girleen, now? Thanks for coming sitting next to me. It's meant something to me, it has.

Girleen   Any time, Father. Any time.

Girleen *exits.* **Welsh** *stares out front again.*

Welsh (*quietly*)   No, not any time, Girleen. Not any time.

He finishes his pint, puts the glass down, blesses himself and sits there quietly a moment, thinking. Blackout.

Scene Five

Stage in darkness apart from **Welsh***, who recites his letter rapidly.*

Welsh   Dear Valene and Coleman, it is Father Welsh here. I am leaving Leenane for good tonight and I wanted to be saying a few words to you, but I won't be preaching at you for why would I be? It has never worked in the past and it won't work now. All I want to do is be pleading with you as a fella

concerned about ye and yere lives, both in this world and the
next, and the next won't be too long away for ye's if ye keep
going on as mad as ye fecking have been. Coleman, I will not
be speaking here about your murdering of your dad, although
obviously it does concern me, both as a priest and as a person
with even the vaguest moral sense, but that is a matter for your
own conscience, although I hope some day you will realise
what you have done and go seeking forgiveness for it, because
let me tell you this, getting your hairstyle insulted is no just
cause to go murdering someone, in fact it's the worst cause I
did ever hear. But I will leave it at that although the same goes
for you, Valene, for your part in your dad's murdering, and
don't go saying you had no part because you did have a part
and a big part. Going lying that it was an accident just to get
your father's money is just as dark a deed as Coleman's deed, if
not more dark, for Coleman's deed was done out of temper
and spite, whereas your deed was done out of being nothing
but a moncy-grubbing fecking miser with no heart at all, but
I said I would not be preaching at you and I have lost me
thread anyways so I will stop preaching at you and be starting
a new paragraph. (*Pause.*) Like I said, I am leaving tonight, but
I have been thinking about ye non-stop since the night I did
scald me hands there at yeres. Every time the pain does go
through them hands I do think about ye, and let me tell you
this. I would take that pain and pain a thousand times worse,
and bear it with a smile, if only I could restore to ye the love
for each other as brothers ye do so woefully lack, that must
have been there some day. Didn't as gasurs ye love each other?
Or as young men, now? Where did it all go on ye? Don't ye
ever think about it? What I think I think what ye've done is
bury it deep down in ye, under a rack of grudges and hate and
sniping like a pair of fecking oul women. Ye two are like a pair
of fecking oul women, so ye are, arging over fecking Taytos
and stoves and figurines, is an arse-brained argument. But I do
think that yere love is still there under all of that, in fact I'd
go betting everything that's dear to me on it, and may I rot in
hell for ever if I'm wrong. All it is is ye've lived in each other's
pockets the entire of yere lives, and a sad and lonesome
existence it has been, with no women to enter the picture for

either of ye to calm ye down, or anyways not many women or the wrong sort of women, and what's happened the bitterness has gone building up and building up without check, the daily grudges and faults and moans and baby-crimes against each other ye can never seem to step back from and see the love there underneath and forgive each other for. Now, what the point of me letter is, couldn't ye do something about it? Couldn't the both of ye, now, go stepping back and be making a listeen of all the things about the other that do get on yere nerves, and the wrongs the other has done all down through the years that you still hold against him, and be reading them lists out, and be discussing them openly, and be taking a deep breath then and be forgiving each other them wrongs, no matter what they may be? Would that be so awful hard, now? It would for ye two, I know, but couldn't ye just be trying it, now? And if it doesn't work it doesn't work, but at least ye could say ye'd tried and would ye be any worse off? And if ye wouldn't be doing it for yourselves, wouldn't ye be doing it for me, now? For a friend of yeres, who cares about ye, who doesn't want to see ye blowing the brains out of each other, who never achieved anything as a priest in Leenane, in fact the opposite, and who'd see ye two becoming true brothers again as the greatest achievement of his whole time here. Sure it would be bordering on the miraculous. I might be canonised after. (*Pause.*) Valene and Coleman, I'm betting everything on ye. I know for sure there's love there somewheres, it's just a case of ye stepping back and looking for it. I'd be willing to bet me own soul that that love is there, and I know well the odds are stacked against me. They're probably 64,000 to one be this time, but I'd go betting on ye's still, for despite everything, despite yere murder and yere mayhem and yere miserliness that'd tear the teeth out of broken goats, I have faith in ye. You wouldn't be letting me down now, would ye? Yours sincerely, and yours with the love of Christ now, Roderick Welsh.

Pause. **Welsh** *shivers slightly. Blackout.*

Scene Six

Valene's *house. Shotgun back on wall, over shelf full of new ceramic figurines, all marked with a 'V'.* **Coleman**, *in glasses, sits in the armchair left, glass of poteen beside him, perusing another women's magazine.* **Valene** *enters carrying a bag and places his hand on the stove in a number of places. Irritated,* **Coleman** *tries to ignore him.*

Valene   I'm checking. (*Pause.*) It's good to have a little check. (*Pause.*) *I* think it is, d'you know? (*Pause.*) Just a *little* check. D'you know what I mean, like?

After a while more of this, **Valene** *takes some new ceramic figurines out of his bag, which he arranges with the others on the shelf.*

Coleman   Ah for . . .

Valene   Eh?

Coleman   Eh?

Valene   Now then, eh?

Coleman   Uh-huh?

Valene   Eh? Nice, I think. Eh? What do *you* think, Coleman?

Coleman   I think you can go feck yourself.

Valene   No, not feck meself at all, now. Or over to the left a biteen would they look better? Hmm, we'll put the new St Martin over here, so it balances out with the other St Martin over there, so's we have one darkie saint on either side, so it balances out symmetrical, like. (*Pause.*) I'm a great one for shelf arranging I am. It is a skill I did never know I had. (*Pause.*) Forty-six figurines now. I'm sure to be getting into heaven with this many figurines in me house.

Valene *finds his pen and marks up the new figurines.*

Coleman (*pause*)   There's a poor girl born in Norway here with no lips.

Valene (*pause*)   That's old news that lip girl is.

Coleman   That girl'll never be getting kissed. Not with the bare gums on her flapping.

Valene   She's the exact same as you, so, if she'll never be getting kissed, and you've no excuse. You've the full complement of lips.

Coleman   I suppose a million girls you've kissed in your time. Oh aye.

Valene   Nearer two million.

Coleman   Two million, aye. And all of them aunties when you was twelve.

Valene   Not aunties at all. Proper women.

Coleman   Me brother Valentine does be living in his own little dream-world, with the sparrows and the fairies and the hairy little men. Puw-ooh! And the daisy people.

Valene (*pause*)   I hope that's not my poteen.

Coleman   It's not at all your poteen.

Valene   Uh-huh? (*Pause.*) Did you hear the news?

Coleman   I did. Isn't it awful?

Valene   It's a disgrace. It's an outright disgrace, and nothing but. You can't go sending off an entire girls' football team, sure.

Coleman   Not in a semi-fecking-final anyways.

Valene   Not at any time, sure. If you have to send people off you send them off one at a time, for their individual offences. You don't go slinging the lot of them off wholesale, and only seven minutes in, so they go crying home to their mammies.

Coleman   St Josephine's have only got through be default, and nothing but default. If they had any honour they'd not take their place in the final at all and be giving it to us.

Valene   I hope they lose the final.

Coleman The same as that, *I* hope they lose the final. Sure, with their goalie in a coma they're bound to.

Valene No, their goalie came out of her coma a while ago there. Intensive care is all she's in now.

Coleman She was fecking feigning? Getting us expelled from all competitions for no reason at all? I hope she relapses into her coma and dies.

Valene The same as that, I hope she lapses into her coma and dies. (*Pause.*) Look at us, we're in agreement.

Coleman We are, I suppose.

Valene We can agree sometimes.

He snatches the magazine out of **Coleman**'*s hands.*

Valene Except don't go reading me magazines, I've told you, till I've finished reading them.

He sits at the table and flips through the magazine without reading it. **Coleman** *fumes.*

Coleman (*standing*) And don't go . . . don't go tearing them out of me fecking hands, near tore the fingers off me!

Valene Have these fingers you (*V sign*) and take them to bed with ya.

Coleman You're not even reading that *Take a Break*.

Valene I *am* reading this *Take a Break*, or anyways I'm glancing through this *Take a Break* at me own pace, as a fella's free to do if it's with his own money he goes buying his *Take a Break*.

Coleman Only women's magazines is all you ever go reading. Sure without doubt it's a fecking gayboy you must be.

Valene There's a lad here in Bosnia and not only has he no arms but his mammy's just died. (*Mumbles as he reads, then:*) Ah they're only after fecking money, the same as ever.

Coleman And no fear of you sending that poor no-armed boy any money, ah no.

Valene   They've probably only got him to put his arms behind his back, just to cod ya.

Coleman   It's any excuse for you.

Valene   And I bet his mammy's fine.

Coleman (*pause*)   Get *Bella* if you're getting magazines. *Take a Break*'s nothing but quizzes.

Valene   There's a coupon here for Honey Nut Loops.

Valene *starts carefully tearing out the coupon at the same time as* **Coleman** *quietly takes some Taytos out of a cupboard.*

Coleman   Quizzes and deformed orphans. (*Pause.*) Em, would you let me be having a bag of Taytos, Val? I'm hungry a biteen.

Valene (*looking up. Pause*)   Are you being serious, now?

Coleman   G'wan. I'll owe you for them.

Valene   Put that bag back, now.

Coleman   I'll owe you for them, I'm saying. You can put them on the same bill you've put your melted figurines.

Valene   Put them . . . put them . . . What are you doing, now? Put them Taytos back, I said.

Coleman   Valene, listen to me . . .

Valene   No . . .

Coleman   I'm hungry and I need some Taytos. Didn't I wait till you came back in to ask you, now, and only because I'm honest . . .

Valene   And you've asked me and I've said no. Slinging insults at me Taytos the other week I remember is all you were. I see the boot's on the other foot now.

Coleman   I've asked polite, now, Valene, and feck boots. Three times I've asked polite.

Valene   I know well you've asked polite, Coleman. You've asked awful polite. And what I'm saying to ya, ya can't have any of me fecking Taytos, now!

Coleman   Is that your final word on the subject?

Valene   It *is* me final word on the subject.

Coleman (*pause*)   I won't have any of your Taytos so. (*Pause.*) I'll just crush them to skitter.

He crushes the crisps to pulp and tosses the packet at **Valene**. **Valene** *darts up and around the table to get at* **Coleman**, *during which time* **Coleman** *grabs two more packets from the cupboard and holds them up, one in each hand, threatening to crush them also.*

Coleman   Back off!

Valene *stops dead in his tracks.*

Coleman   Back off or they'll be getting it the camel

Valene (*scared*)   Be leaving me crisps now, Coleman.

Coleman   Be leaving them, is it? When all I wanted was to go buying one of them and would've paid the full whack, but oh no.

Valene (*tearfully, choking*)   That's a waste of good food that is, Coleman.

Coleman   Good food, is it?

Valene   There's Bosnians'd be happy to have them Taytos.

Coleman *opens one of the bags and starts eating just as the front door bangs open and* **Girleen** *enters, face blotchy, letter in hand.*

Coleman   They *are* good food, d'you know?

Girleen (*in shock throughout*)   Have ye heard the news, now?

Coleman   What news, Girleen? The under-twelves . . . ?

Seeing **Coleman** *distracted,* **Valene** *dives for his neck, trying to get the crisps off him at the same time. They drag each other to the floor, rolling and scuffling,* **Coleman** *purposely mashing up the crisps any chance he gets.* **Girleen** *stares at them a while, then quietly takes a butcher's knife out of one of the drawers, goes over to them, pulls* **Coleman**'s *head back by the hair and puts the knife to his neck.*

Valene   Leave Coleman alone, Girleen. What are you doing, now?

Girleen   I'm breaking ye up.

Coleman (*scared*)   We're broke up.

Valene (*scared*)   We're broke up.

Once the two are separated, **Girleen** *lets* **Coleman** *go and puts the letter on the table, sadly.*

Girleen   There's a letter there Father Welsh wrote ye.

Valene   What does that feck want writing to us?

Coleman   Going moaning again, I'll bet.

Valene *picks the letter up,* **Coleman** *pulls it off him,* **Valene** *pulls it back. They stand reading it together,* **Coleman** *getting bored after a few seconds.* **Girleen** *takes out a heart pendant on a chain and looks at it.*

Girleen   I read it already on ye, coming over. All about the two of ye loving each other as brothers it is.

Coleman (*stifling laughter*)   Wha?

Valene   Father Walsh Welsh's leaving, it looks like.

Coleman   Is it full of moaning, Valene? It is.

Valene   And nothing but moaning. (*Mimicking.*) 'Getting your hairstyle insulted is no just cause to go murdering someone, in fact it's the worst cause I did ever hear.'

Coleman (*laughing*)   That was a funny voice.

Girleen   I did order him this heart on a chain out of me mam's Freeman's catalogue. Only this morning it came. I asked him to be writing me with his new address last night, so I could send it on to him. I'd've never've got up the courage to be giving it him to his face. I'd've blushed the heart out of me. Four months I've been saving up to buy it him. All me poteen money. (*Crying.*) All me poteen money gone. I should've skittered it away the boys in Carraroe, and not go pinning me hopes on a feck I knew full well I'd never have.

Girleen *cuts the chain in two with the knife.*

Coleman   Don't be cutting your good chain there, Girleen.

Valene   Be leaving your chaineen there now, Girleen. That chain looks worth something.

Girleen *tosses the chain in a corner.*

Girleen (*sniffling*)   Have you read the letter there, now?

Valene   I have. A pile of oul bull.

Girleen   I read it to see if he mentioned me. Not a word.

Coleman   Just shite is it, Valene? It's not worth reading?

Valene   Not at all.

Coleman   I'll leave it so, for I've no time for letters. I've never seen the sense in them. They're just writing.

Girleen   I did like the bit about him betting his soul on ye. Didn't ye like that bit?

Valene *picks up the broken chain.*

Valene   I don't think I understood that bit.

Girleen (*pause*)   Father Welsh drowned himself in the lake last night, same place as Tom Hanlon. They dragged his body out this morning. His soul in hell he's talking about, that only ye can save for him. (*Pause.*) You notice he never asked me to go saving his soul. I'd've liked to've saved his soul. I'd've been honoured, but no. (*Crying*) Only mad drunken pig-shite feck-brained thicks he goes asking.

Shocked, **Coleman** *reads the letter.* **Girleen** *goes to the door.* **Valene** *offers the pendant out to her.*

Valene   Your heart, Girleen, be keeping it for yourself.

Girleen (*crying*)   Feck me heart. Feck it to hell. Toss it into fecking skitter's the best place for that fecking heart. (*Exiting*) Not even a word to me!

After **Girleen** *exits,* **Valene** *sits in an armchair, looking at the chain.* **Coleman** *finishes reading the letter, leaves it on the table and sits in the opposite armchair.*

Valene   Did you read it?

Coleman   I did.

Valene (*pause*)   Isn't it sad about him?

Coleman   It *is* sad. Very sad.

Valene (*pause*)   Will we be trying for ourselves? To get along, now?

Coleman   We will.

Valene   There's no harm in trying.

Coleman   No harm at all, sure.

Valene (*pause*)   Poor Father Welsh Walsh Welsh.

Coleman   Welsh.

Valene   Welsh. (*Pause.*) I wonder why he did it?

Coleman   I suppose he must've been upset o'er something.

Valene   I suppose. (*Pause.*) This is a pricey chain. (*Pause.*) We'll be giving it back to her next time we see her. She's only shocked now.

Coleman   Aye. She's not in her right mind at all. She did hurt me hair when she tugged at it too, d'you know?

Valene   It did look like it hurt.

Coleman   It did hurt.

Valene (*pause*)   Father Welsh going topping himself does put arging o'er Taytos into perspective anyways.

Coleman   It does.

Valene   Eh?

Coleman   It does.

Valene   Aye. Awful perspective. Awful perspective.

Coleman (*pause*)   Did you see 'Roderick' his name is?

Valene (*snorts*)   I did.

Coleman (*pause. Seriously*)   We shouldn't laugh.

Valene *nods. Both pull serious faces. Blackout.*

Scene Seven

Room tidier. **Welsh**'s *letter pinned to the foot of the crucifix.* **Valene**
and **Coleman** *enter dressed in black, having just attended* **Welsh**'s
funeral, **Coleman** *carrying a small plastic bag full of sausage rolls and
vol-au-vents. He sits at the table.* **Valene** *opens his poteen biscuit tin.*

Valene   That's that, then.

Coleman   That's that, aye. That's Father Welsh gone.

Valene   A good do.

Coleman   Aye. It's often a good do when it's a priest they're
sticking away.

He empties his bag onto table.

Valene   You didn't have to go nabbing a whole bagful, now,
Coleman.

Coleman   Didn't they offer, sure?

Valene   But a whole bagful, I'm saying.

Coleman   It'd have only gone to waste, and sure a bagful
won't be going very far between us.

Valene   Between us?

Coleman   Of course between us.

Valene   Ohh.

They both eat a little.

These are nice vol-au-vents.

Coleman   They *are* nice vol-au-vents.

Valene   You can't say the Catholic Church doesn't know
how to make a nice vol-au-vent, now.

Coleman   It's their best feature. And their sausage rolls
aren't bad either, although they probably only buy them in.

Valene (*pause*)   Em, would you be having a glass of poteen
with me, Coleman?

Coleman (*shocked*)   I would, now. If you can spare a drop, like.

Valene   I can easy spare a drop.

Valene *pours two glasses, one bigger than the other, thinks about it, then gives* **Coleman** *the bigger.*

Coleman   Thank you, Valene. Sure we have our own little feasteen now.

Valene   We do.

Coleman   D'you remember when as gasurs we did used to put the blankets o'er the gap between our beds and hide under them like a tent it was o'er us, and go having a feasteen of oul jammy sandwiches then?

Valene   That was you and Mick Dowd used to go camping in the gap between our beds. You'd never let me be in with yous at all. Ye used to step on me head if I tried to climb into that camp with you. I still remember it.

Coleman   Mick Dowd, was it? I don't remember that at all, now. I did think it was you.

Valene   Half me childhood you spent stepping on me head, and for no reason. And d'you remember when you pinned me down and sat across me on me birthday and let the stringy spit dribble out your gob and let down and down it dribble till it landed in me eye then?

Coleman   I remember it well, Valene, and I'll tell you this. I did mean to suck that spit back up just before it got to your eye, but what happened I lost control o'er it.

Valene   And on me birthday.

Coleman (*pause*)   I do apologise for dribbling in your eye and I do apologise for stepping on your head, Valene. On Father Welsh's soul I apologise.

Valene   I do accept your apology so.

Coleman Although plenty of times as a gasur I remember you dropping stones on me head while I was asleep and big stones.

Valene Only in retaliation them stones ever was.

Coleman Retaliation or not. Waking up to stones dropped on ya is awful frightening for a small child. And retaliation doesn't count anyways if it's a week later. It's only then and there retaliation does apply.

Valene I do apologise for dropping stones on you so. (*Pause.*) For your brain never did recover from them injuries, did it, Coleman?

Coleman *stares at* **Valene** *a second, then smiles.* **Valene** *smiles also.*

Valene This is a great oul game, this is, apologising. Father Welsh wasn't too far wrong.

Coleman I hope Father Welsh isn't in hell at all. I hope he's in heaven.

Valene *I* hope he's in heaven.

Coleman Or purgatory at worst.

Valene Although if he's in hell at least he'll have Tom Hanlon to speak to.

Coleman So it won't be as if he doesn't know anybody.

Valene Aye. And the fella off *Alias Smith and Jones.*

Coleman Is the fella off *Alias Smith and Jones* in hell?

Valene He is. Father Welsh was telling me.

Coleman The blond one.

Valene No, the other one.

Coleman He was good, the other one.

Valene He was the best one.

Coleman It's always the best ones go to hell. Me, probably straight to heaven I'll go, even though I blew the head off poor

Dad. So long as I go confessing to it anyways. That's the good thing about being Catholic. You can shoot your dad in the head and it doesn't even matter at all.

Valene   Well, it matters a little bit.

Coleman   It matters a little bit but not a big bit.

Valene (*pause*)   Did you see Girleen crying her eyes out, the funeral?

Coleman   I did.

Valene   Poor Girleen. And her mam two times has had to drag her screaming from the lake at night, did you hear, there where Father Walsh jumped, and her just standing there, staring.

Coleman   She must've liked Father Welsh or something.

Valene   I suppose she must've. (*Taking out* **Girleen**'s *chain.*) She wouldn't take her chaineen back at all. She wouldn't hear tell of it. I'll put it up here with his letter to us.

He attaches the chain to the cross, so the heart rests on the letter, which he gently smoothes out.

It's the mental they'll be putting Girleen in before long if she carries on.

Coleman   Sure it's only a matter of time.

Valene   Isn't that sad?

Coleman   Awful sad. (*Pause. Shrugging.*) Ah well.

He eats another vol-au-vent. **Valene** *remembers something, fishes in the pockets of his jacket, takes out two ceramic figurines, places them on the shelf, uncaps his pen almost automatically, thinks better of marking them as before, and puts the pen away.*

Coleman   I think I'm getting to like vol-au-vents now. I think I'm developing a taste for them. We ought to go to more funerals.

Valene   They do have them at weddings too.

Coleman   Do they? Who'll next be getting married round here so? Girleen I would used to have said, as pretty as she is, only she'll probably have topped herself before ever she gets married.

Valene   *Me* probably'll be the next one getting married, as handsome as I am. Did you see today all the young nuns eyeing me?

Coleman   Who'd go marrying you, sure? Even that no-lipped girl in Norway'd turn you down.

Valene (*pause. Angrily*)   See, I'm stepping back now . . . I'm stepping back, like Father Walsh said, and I'm forgiving ya, insulting me.

Coleman (*sincerely*)   Oh . . . oh, I'm sorry now, Valene. I'm sorry. It just slipped out on me without thinking.

Valene   No harm done so, if only an accident it was.

Coleman   It *was* an accident. Although remember you did insult me there earlier, saying I was brain-damaged be stones as a gasur, and I didn't even pull you up on it.

Valene   I apologise for saying you was brain-damaged as a gasur so.

Coleman   No apology was necessary, Valene, and I have saved you the last vol-au-venteen on top of it.

Valene   You have that last vol-au-vent, Coleman. I'm not overly keen on vol-au-vents.

Coleman *nods in thanks and eats the vol-au-vent.*

Valene   Weren't them young nuns lovely today now, Coleman?

Coleman   They was lovely nuns.

Valene   They must've known Father Welsh from nun college or something.

Coleman   I'd like to touch them nuns both upstairs and downstairs, so I would. Except for the fat one on the end.

Valene   She was a horror and she knew.

Coleman   If Dad was there today he'd've just gone screaming at them nuns.

Valene   Why *did* Dad used to go screaming at nuns, Coleman?

Coleman   I don't have an idea at all why he used to scream at nuns. He must've had a bad experience with nuns as a child.

Valene   If you hadn't blown the brains out of Dad we could ask him outright.

Coleman *stares at him sternly.*

Valene   No, I'm not saying anything, now. I'm calm, I've stepped back, and I'm saying this quietly and without any spite at all, but you know well that that wasn't right, Coleman, shooting Dad in the head on us. In your heart anyways you know.

Coleman (*pause*)   I *do* know it wasn't right. Not only in me heart but in me head and in me everywhere. I was wrong for shooting Dad. I was dead wrong. And I'm sorry for it.

Valene   And I'm sorry for sitting you down and making you sign your life away, Coleman. It was the only way at the time I could think of punishing ya. Well, I could've let you go to jail but I didn't want you going to jail and it wasn't out of miserliness that I stopped you going to jail. It was more out of I didn't want all on me own to be left here. I'd've missed ya. (*Pause.*) From this day on . . . from this day on, this house and everything in this house is half yours again, Coleman.

Touched, **Coleman** *offers his hand out and they shake, embarrassed. Pause.*

Valene   Is there any other confessions we have to get off our chests, now we're at it?

Coleman   There must be millions. (*Pause.*) Crushing your crisps to skitter, Valene, I'm sorry for.

Valene   I forgive you for it. (*Pause.*) Do you remember that holiday in Lettermullen as gasurs we had, and you left your cowboy stagecoach out in the rain that night and next morning it was gone and Mam and Dad said, 'Oh it must've been hijacked be Indians.' It wasn't hijacked be Indians. I'd got up early and pegged it in the sea.

Coleman (*pause*)   I did love that cowboy stagecoach.

Valene   I know you did, and I'm sorry for it.

Coleman (*pause*)   That string of gob I dribbled on you on your birthday. I didn't try to suck it back up at all. I wanted it to hit your eye and I was glad. (*Pause.*) And I'm sorry for it.

Valene   Okay. (*Pause.*) Maureen Folan did once ask me to ask you if you wanted to see a film at the Claddagh Palace with her, and she'd've driven ye and paid for dinner too, and from the tone of her voice it sounded like you'd've been on a promise after, but I never passed the message onto ya, out of nothing but pure spite.

Coleman   Sure that's no great loss, Valene. Maureen Folan looks like a thin-lipped ghost, with the hairstyle of a frightened red ape.

Valene   But on a promise you'd've been.

Coleman   On a promise or no. That was nothing at all to go confessing. Okay, it's my go. I'm winning.

Valene   What d'you mean, you're winning?

Coleman (*thinking*)   Do you remember your Ker-Plunk game?

Valene   I *do* remember me Ker-Plunk game.

Coleman   It wasn't Liam Hanlon stole all them marbles out of your Ker-Plunk game at all, it was me.

Valene   What did you want me Ker-Plunk marbles for?

Coleman   I went slinging them at the swans in Galway. I had a great time.

Valene   That ruined me Ker-Plunk. You can't play Ker-Plunk without marbles. And, sure, that was *both* of ours Ker-Plunk.

That was just cutting off your nose to spite your face, Coleman.

Coleman   I know it was and I'm sorry, Valene. Your go now. (*Pause.*) You're too slow. D'you remember when we had them backward children staying for B & B, and they threw half your *Spider Man* comics in on the fire? They didn't. D'you know who did? I did. I only blamed them cos they were too daft to arg.

Valene   They was good *Spider Man* comics, Coleman. Spider Man went fighting Doctor Octopus in them comics.

Coleman   And I'm sorry for it. Your go. (*Pause.*) You're too slow . . .

Valene   Hey . . . !

Coleman   D'you remember when Pato Dooley beat the skitter out of you when he was twelve and you was twenty, and you never knew the reason why? I knew the reason why. I did tell him you'd called his dead mammy a hairy whore.

Valene   With a fecking chisel that Pato Dooley beat me up that day! Almost had me fecking eye out!

Coleman   I think Pato must've liked his mammy or something. (*Pause.*) I'm awful sorry for it, Valene.

He burps lazily.

Valene   You do sound it!

Coleman   Shall I be having another go?

Valene   I did pour a cup of piss in a pint of lager you drank one time, Coleman. Aye, and d'you know what, now? You couldn't even tell the differ.

Coleman (*pause*)   When was this, now?

Valene   When you was seventeen, this was. D'you remember that month you were laid up in hospital with bacterial tonsilitis. Around then it was. (*Pause.*) And I'm sorry for it, Coleman.

Coleman I do take your poteen out its box each week, drink the half of it and fill the rest back up with water. Ten years this has been going on. You haven't tasted full-strength poteen since nineteen eighty-fecking-three.

Valene (*drinks. Pause*) But you're sorry for it.

Coleman I suppose I'm sorry for it, aye. (*Mumbling.*) Making me go drinking piss, and not just anybody's piss but *your* fecking piss . . .

Valene (*angrily*) But you're sorry for it, you're saying?!

Coleman I'm sorry for it, aye! I'm fecking sorry for it! Haven't I said?!

Valene That's okay, so, if you're sorry for it, although you don't sound fecking sorry for it.

Coleman You can kiss me fecking arse so, Valene, if you don't . . . I'm taking a step back now, so I am. (*Pause.*) I'm sorry for watering your poteen down all these years, Valene. I am, now.

Valene Good-oh (*Pause.*) Is it your go now or is it mine?

Coleman I think it might be your go, Valene.

Valene Thank you, Coleman. D'you remember when Alison O'Hoolihan went sucking that pencil in the playground that time, and ye were to go dancing the next day, but somebody nudged that pencil and it got stuck in her tonsils on her, and be the time she got out of hospital she was engaged to the doctor who wrenched it out for her and wouldn't be giving you a fecking sniffeen. Do you remember, now?

Coleman I do remember.

Valene That was me nudged that pencil, and it wasn't an accident at all. Pure jealous I was.

Pause. **Coleman** *throws his sausage rolls in* **Valene**'s *face and dives over the table for his neck.* **Valene** *dodges the attack.*

Valene   And I'm sorry for it! I'm sorry for it! (*Pointing at letter.*) Father Welsh! Father Welsh!

Valene *fends* **Coleman** *off. They stand staring at each other,* **Coleman** *seething.*

Coleman   Eh?!

Valene   Eh?

Coleman   I did fecking love Alison O'Hoolihan! We may've been married today if it hadn't been for that fecking pencil!

Valene   What was she doing sucking it the pointy-end inwards anyways? She was looking for trouble!

Coleman   And she fecking found it with you! That pencil could've killed Alison O'Hoolihan!

Valene   And I'm sorry for it, I said. What are you doing pegging good sausage rolls at me? Them sausage rolls cost money. You were supposed to have taken a step back and went calming yourself, but you didn't, you just flew off the handle. Father Welsh's soul'll be roasting now because of you.

Coleman   Leave Father Welsh's soul out of it. This is about you sticking pencils down poor girls' gobs on them.

Valene   That pencil is water under a bridge and I've apologised wholehearted for that pencil. (*Sits down.*) And she had boss-eyes anyways.

Coleman   She didn't have boss-eyes! She had nice eyes!

Valene   Well, there was something funny about them.

Coleman   She had nice brown eyes.

Valene   Oh aye. (*Pause.*) Well, it's your go now, Coleman. Try and top that one for yourself. Heh.

Coleman   Try and top that one, is it?

Valene   It is.

Coleman *thinks for a moment, smiles slightly, then sits back down.*

Coleman   I've taken a step back now.

Valene   I can see you've taken a step back.

Coleman   I'm pure calm now. It does be good to get things off your chest.

Valene   It *does* be good. I'm glad that pencil-nudging's off me chest. I can sleep nights now.

Coleman   Is it a relief to ya?

Valene   It *is* a relief to me. (*Pause.*) What have you got cooking up?

Coleman   I have one and I'm terrible sorry for it. Oh terrible sorry I am.

Valene   It won't be near as good as me pencilling poor boss-eyed Alison, whatever it is.

Coleman   Ah I suppose you're right, now. My one's only a weeny oul one. D'you remember you always thought it was Mairtin Hanlon snipped the ears off of poor Lassie, now?

Valene (*confidently*)   I don't believe you at all. You're only making it up now, see.

Coleman   It wasn't wee Mairtin at all. D'you know who it was, now?

Valene   Me arse was it you. You'll have to be doing better than that, now, Coleman.

Coleman   To the brookeen I dragged him, me scissors in hand, and him whimpering his fat gob off 'til the deed was done and he dropped down dead with not a fecking peep out of that whiny fecking dog.

Valene   D'you see, it doesn't hurt me at all when you go making up lies. You don't understand the rules, Coleman. It does have to be true, else it's just plain daft. You can't go claiming credit for snipping the ears off a dog when you didn't lay a finger on that dog's ears, and the fecking world knows.

Coleman (*pause*)   Is it evidence, so, you're after?

Valene   It *is* evidence I'm after, aye. Go bring me evidence you did cut the ears off me dog. And be quick with that evidence.

Coleman   I won't be quick at all. I will take me time.

He slowly gets up and ambles to his room, closing its door behind him. **Valene** *waits patiently, giving a worried laugh. After a ten-second pause,* **Coleman** *ambles back on, carrying a slightly wet brown paper bag. He pauses at the table a moment for dramatic effect, slowly opens the bag, pulls out a dog's big fluffy black ear, lays it on top of* **Valene***'s head, takes out the second ear, pauses, places that on* **Valene***'s head also, puts the empty bag down on the table, smoothes it out, then sits down in the armchair left.* **Valene** *has been staring out into space all the while, dumbstruck. He tilts his head so that the ears fall down onto the table, and he stares at them a while.* **Coleman** *picks up* **Valene***'s felt-tip pen, brings it over and lays it on the table.*

Coleman   There's your little peneen, now, Val. Why don't you mark them dog's ears with your V, so we'll be remembering who they belong to.

He sits back down in the armchair.

And do you want to hear something else, Valene? I'm sorry for cutting off them dog's ears. With all me fecking heart I'm sorry, oh aye, because I've tooken a step back now, look at me . . .

He half laughs through his nose. **Valene** *gets up, stares blankly at* **Coleman** *a moment, goes to the cupboard right and, with his back to* **Coleman***, pulls the butcher's knife out of it. In the same brief second* **Coleman** *stands, pulls the shotgun down from above the stove and sits down with it.* **Valene** *turns, knife ready. The gun is pointed directly at him.* **Valene** *wilts slightly, thinks about it a moment, regains his courage and his anger, and slowly approaches* **Coleman***, raising the knife.*

Coleman (*surprised, slightly scared*)   What are you doing, now, Valene?

Valene (*blankly*)   Oh not a thing am I doing, Coleman, other than killing ya.

Coleman   Be putting that knife back in that drawer, you.

Valene   No, I'll be putting it in the head of you, now.

Coleman   Don't you see me gun?

Valene   Me poor fecking Lassie, who never hurt a flea.

He has gotten all the way up to **Coleman**, *so that the barrel of the gun is touching his chest. He raises the knife to its highest point.*

Coleman   What are you doing, now? Stop it.

Valene   I'll stop it, all right . . .

Coleman   Father Welsh's soul, Valene. Father Wel—

Valene   Father Welsh's soul me fecking arse! Father Welsh's soul didn't come into play when you hacked me dog's ears off him and kept them in a bag!

Coleman   Ar that was a year ago. How does that apply?

Valene   Be saying goodbye to the world, you, ya feck!

Coleman   *You'll* have to be saying goodbye to the world too, so, because I'll be bringing you with me.

Valene   Do I look like I mind that at all, now?

Coleman (*pause*)   Er er, wait wait wait, now . . .

Valene   Wha . . . ?

Coleman   Look at me gun. Look at me gun where it's going, do ya see. . . ?

Coleman *slides the gun away and down from* **Valene**'s *chest till it points directly at the door of the stove.*

Valene (*pause*)   Be pointing that gun away from me stove, now.

Coleman   I won't be. Stab away, now. It's your stove it'll be'll be going with me instead of ya.

Valene   Leave . . . what . . . ? That was a three-hundred-pound stove now, Coleman . . .

Coleman   I know well it was.

Valene   Be leaving it alone. That's just being sly, that is.

Coleman   Be backing off you with that knife, you sissy-arse.

Valene (*tearfully*)   You're not a man at all, pointing guns at stoves.

Coleman   I don't care if I am or I'm not. Be backing off, I said.

Valene   You're just a . . . you're just a . . .

Coleman   Eh?

Valene   Eh?

Coleman   Eh?

Valene   You're not a man at all, you.

Coleman   Be backing away now, you, crybaby. Be taking a step back for yourself. Eheh.

Valene (*pause*)   I'm backing away now, so I am.

Coleman   That'd be the best thing, aye.

Valene *slowly retreats, lays the knife on the table and sits down there sadly, gently stroking his dog's ears.* **Coleman** *is still pointing the gun at the stove door. He shakes his head slightly.*

Coleman   I can't believe you raised a knife to me. No, I can't believe you raised a knife to your own brother.

Valene   You raised a knife to me own dog and raised a gun to our own father, did a lot more damage than a fecking knife, now.

Coleman   No, I can't believe it. I can't believe you raised a knife to me.

Valene   Stop going on about raising a knife, and be pointing that gun away from me fecking stove, now, in case it does go off be accident.

Coleman   Be accident, is it?

Valene   Is the safety catch on that gun, now?

Coleman   The safety catch, is it?

Valene   Aye, the safety catch! The safety catch! Is it ten million times I have to be repeating meself?

Coleman   The safety catch, uh-huh . . .

He jumps to his feet, points the gun down at the stove and fires, blowing the right-hand side apart. **Valene** *falls to his knees in horror, his face in his hands.* **Coleman** *cocks the gun again and blows the left-hand side apart also, then nonchalantly sits back down.*

Coleman   No, the safety catch isn't on at all, Valene. Would you believe it?

Pause. **Valene** *is still kneeling there, dumbstruck.*

Coleman   And I'll tell you another thing . . .

He suddenly jumps up again and, holding the shotgun by the barrel, starts smashing it violently into the figurines, shattering them to pieces and sending them flying around the room until not a single one remains standing. **Valene** *screams throughout. After* **Coleman** *has finished he sits again, the gun across his lap.* **Valene** *is still kneeling. Pause.*

Coleman   And don't go making out that you didn't deserve it, because we both know full well that you did.

Valene (*numbly*)   You've broken all me figurines, Coleman.

Coleman   I have. Did you see me?

Valene   And you've blown me stove to buggery.

Coleman   This is a great gun for blowing holes in things.

Valene (*standing*)   And now you do have no bullets left in that great gun.

He lazily picks the knife back up and approaches **Coleman**. *But as he does so* **Coleman** *opens the barrel of the gun, tosses away the spent cartridges, fishes in his pocket, comes out with a clenched fist that may or may not contain another cartridge, shows the fist to* **Valene** . . .

Valene   There's no bullet in that hand! There's no bullet in that hand!

. . . and loads, or pretends to load, the bullet into the gun, without **Valene** *or the audience at any time knowing if there is a bullet or not.* **Coleman** *snaps the barrel shut and lazily points it at* **Valene**'s *head.*

Coleman *cocks the gun. Long, long pause.*

Valene   I want to kill you, Coleman.

Coleman   Ar, don't be saying that, now, Val.

Valene (*sadly*)   It's true, Coleman. I want to kill you.

Coleman (*pause*)   Try so.

Pause. **Valene** *turns the knife around and around in his hand, staring at* **Coleman** *all the while, until his head finally droops and he returns the knife to the drawer.* **Coleman** *uncocks the gun, stands, and lays it down on the table, staying near it.* **Valene** *idles to the stove and touches the letter pinned above it.*

Valene   Father Welsh is burning in hell, now, because of our fighting.

Coleman   Well, did we ask him to go betting his soul on us? No. And, sure, it's pure against the rules for priests to go betting anyways, never minding with them kinds of stakes. Sure a fiver would've been overdoing it on us, let alone his soul. And what's wrong with fighting anyways? I do like a good fight. It does show you care, fighting does. That's what oul sissy Welsh doesn't understand. Don't you like a good fight?

Valene   I *do* like a good fight, the same as that. Although I don't like having me dog murdered on me, and me fecking dad murdered on me.

Coleman   And I'm sorry for your dog and Dad, Valene. I *am* sorry. Truly I'm sorry. And nothing to do with Father Welsh's letter is this at all. From me own heart this is. The same goes for your stove and your poor figurines too. Look at them. That was pure temper, that was. Although, admit it, you asked for that stove and them figurines.

Valene   You never fecking stop, you. (*Pause.*) *Are* you sorry, Coleman?

Coleman   I am, Valene.

Valene (*pause*)   Maybe Father Walsh's Welsh's soul'll be all right so.

Coleman   Maybe it will, now. Maybe it will.

Valene   He wasn't such a bad fella.

Coleman   He wasn't.

Valene   He wasn't a great fella, but he wasn't a bad fella.

Coleman   Aye. (*Pause.*) He was a *middling* fella.

Valene   He was a *middling* fella.

Coleman (*pause*)   I'm going out for a drink for meself. Will you be coming with me?

Valene   Aye, in a minute now I'll come.

Coleman *goes to the front door.* **Valene** *looks over the smashed figurines sadly.*

Coleman   I'll help you be clearing your figurines up when I get back, Valene. Maybe we can glue some of them together. Do you still have your superglue?

Valene   I do have me superglue, although I think the top's gone hard.

Coleman   Aye, that's the trouble with superglue.

Valene   Ah, the house insurance'll cover me figurines anyways. As well as me stove.

Coleman   Oh . . .

Valene (*pause*)   What, oh?

Coleman   Do you remember a couple of weeks ago there when you asked me did I go stealing your insurance money and I said no, I paid it in for you?

Valene   I do remember.

Coleman (*pause*)   I didn't pay it in at all. I pocketed the lot of it, pissed it up a wall.

Valene, *seething, darts for the knife drawer.* **Coleman** *dashes out through the front door, slamming it behind him.* **Valene** *tosses the knife away, darts back to the gun and brings it to the door.* **Coleman** *is long gone. Gun in hand,* **Valene** *stands there, shaking with rage, almost in tears. After a while he begins to calm down, taking deep breaths. He looks down at the gun in his hands a moment, then gently opens the barrel to see if* **Coleman** *had really loaded it earlier. He had.* **Valene** *takes the cartridge out.*

Valene   He'd've fecking shot me too. He'd've shot his own fecking brother! On top of his dad! On top of me stove!

He tosses the gun and cartridge away, rips **Father Welsh**'*s letter off the cross, knocking* **Girleen**'*s chain onto the floor, brings the letter back to the table and takes out a box of matches.*

Valene   And you, you whiny fecking priest. Do I need your soul hovering o'er me the rest of me fecking life? How could anybody be getting on with that feck?

He strikes a match and lights the letter, which he glances over as he holds up. After a couple of seconds, the letter barely singed, he blows the flames out and looks at it on the table, sighing.

(*Quietly.*) I'm too fecking kind-hearted is my fecking trouble.

He returns to the cross and pins the chain and letter back onto it, smoothing the letter out. He puts on his jacket, checks it for loose change and goes to the front door.

Well, I won't be buying the fecker a pint anyways. I'll tell you that for nothing, Father Welsh Walsh Welsh.

Valene *glances back at the letter a second, sadly, looks down at the floor, then exits. Lights fade, with one light lingering on the crucifix and letter a half-second longer than the others.*

Methuen Drama Modern Classics

Jean Anouilh *Antigone* • Brendan Behan *The Hostage* • Robert Bolt *A Man for All Seasons* • Edward Bond *Saved* • Bertolt Brecht *The Caucasian Chalk Circle* • *Fear and Misery in the Third Reich* • *The Good Person of Szechwan* • *Life of Galileo* • *The Messingkauf Dialogues* • *Mother Courage and Her Children* • *Mr Puntila and His Man Matti* • *The Resistible Rise of Arturo Ui* • *Rise and Fall of the City of Mahagonny* • *The Threepenny Opera* • Jim Cartwright *Road* • *Two & Bed* • Caryl Churchill *Serious Money* • *Top Girls* • Noël Coward *Blithe Spirit* • *Hay Fever* • *Present Laughter* • *Private Lives* • *The Vortex* • Shelagh Delaney *A Taste of Honey* • Dario Fo *Accidental Death of an Anarchist* • Michael Frayn *Copenhagen* • Lorraine Hansberry *A Raisin in the Sun* • Jonathan Harvey *Beautiful Thing* • David Mamet *Glengarry Glen Ross* • *Oleanna* • *Speed-the-Plow* • Patrick Marber *Closer* • *Dealer's Choice* • Arthur Miller *Broken Glass* • Percy Mtwa, Mbongeni Ngema, Barney Simon *Woza Albert!* • Joe Orton *Entertaining Mr Sloane* • *Loot* • *What the Butler Saw* • Mark Ravenhill *Shopping and F***ing* • Willy Russell *Blood Brothers* • *Educating Rita* • *Stags and Hens* • *Our Day Out* • Jean-Paul Sartre *Crime Passionnel* • Wole Soyinka • *Death and the King's Horseman* • Theatre Workshop *Oh, What a Lovely War* • Frank Wedekind • *Spring Awakening* • Timberlake Wertenbaker *Our Country's Good*

Methuen Drama Student Editions

Jean Anouilh *Antigone* • John Arden *Serjeant Musgrave's Dance*
Alan Ayckbourn *Confusions* • Aphra Behn *The Rover* • Edward Bond
Lear • *Saved* • Bertolt Brecht *The Caucasian Chalk Circle* • *Fear and
Misery in the Third Reich* • *The Good Person of Szechwan* • *Life of Galileo* •
Mother Courage and her Children • *The Resistible Rise of Arturo Ui* • *The
Threepenny Opera* • Anton Chekhov *The Cherry Orchard* • *The Seagull* •
Three Sisters • *Uncle Vanya* • Caryl Churchill *Serious Money* • *Top Girls*
• Shelagh Delaney *A Taste of Honey* • Euripides *Elektra* • *Medea*•
Dario Fo *Accidental Death of an Anarchist* • Michael Frayn *Copenhagen*
• John Galsworthy *Strife* • Nikolai Gogol *The Government Inspector* •
Robert Holman *Across Oka* • Henrik Ibsen *A Doll's House* • *Ghosts*•
Hedda Gabler • Charlotte Keatley *My Mother Said I Never Should* •
Bernard Kops *Dreams of Anne Frank* • Federico García Lorca *Blood
Wedding* • *Doña Rosita the Spinster* (bilingual edition) •*The House of
Bernarda Alba* • (bilingual edition) • *Yerma* (bilingual edition) • David
Mamet *Glengarry Glen Ross* • *Oleanna* • Patrick Marber *Closer* • John
Marston *Malcontent* • Martin McDonagh *The Lieutenant of Inishmore* •
Joe Orton *Loot* • Luigi Pirandello *Six Characters in Search of an Author*
• Mark Ravenhill *Shopping and F***ing* • Willy Russell *Blood Brothers*
• *Educating Rita* • Sophocles *Antigone* • *Oedipus the King* • Wole
Soyinka *Death and the King's Horseman* • Shelagh Stephenson *The
Memory of Water* • August Strindberg *Miss Julie* • J. M. Synge *The
Playboy of the Western World* • Theatre Workshop *Oh What a Lovely
War* Timberlake Wertenbaker *Our Country's Good* • Arnold Wesker
The Merchant • Oscar Wilde *The Importance of Being Earnest* •
Tennessee Williams *A Streetcar Named Desire* • *The Glass Menagerie*

Methuen Drama Contemporary Dramatists

include

John Arden (two volumes)
Arden & D'Arcy
Peter Barnes (three volumes)
Sebastian Barry
Dermot Bolger
Edward Bond (eight volumes)
Howard Brenton
   (two volumes)
Richard Cameron
Jim Cartwright
Caryl Churchill (two volumes)
Sarah Daniels (two volumes)
Nick Darke
David Edgar (three volumes)
David Eldridge
Ben Elton
Dario Fo (two volumes)
Michael Frayn (three volumes)
David Greig
John Godber (four volumes)
Paul Godfrey
John Guare
Lee Hall (two volumes)
Peter Handke
Jonathan Harvey
   (two volumes)
Declan Hughes
Terry Johnson (three volumes)
Sarah Kane
Barrie Keeffe
Bernard-Marie Koltès
   (two volumes)
Franz Xaver Kroetz
David Lan
Bryony Lavery
Deborah Levy
Doug Lucie

David Mamet (four volumes)
Martin McDonagh
Duncan McLean
Anthony Minghella
   (two volumes)
Tom Murphy (six volumes)
Phyllis Nagy
Anthony Neilsen (two volumes)
Philip Osment
Gary Owen
Louise Page
Stewart Parker (two volumes)
Joe Penhall (two volumes)
Stephen Poliakoff
   (three volumes)
David Rabe (two volumes)
Mark Ravenhill (two volumes)
Christina Reid
Philip Ridley
Willy Russell
Eric-Emmanuel Schmitt
Ntozake Shange
Sam Shepard (two volumes)
Wole Soyinka (two volumes)
Simon Stephens (two volumes)
Shelagh Stephenson
David Storey (three volumes)
Sue Townsend
Judy Upton
Michel Vinaver
   (two volumes)
Arnold Wesker (two volumes)
Michael Wilcox
Roy Williams (three volumes)
Snoo Wilson (two volumes)
David Wood (two volumes)
Victoria Wood

Methuen Drama World Classics

include

Jean Anouilh (two volumes)
Brendan Behan
Aphra Behn
Bertolt Brecht (eight volumes)
Büchner
Bulgakov
Calderón
Čapek
Anton Chekhov
Noël Coward (eight volumes)
Feydeau
Eduardo De Filippo
Max Frisch
John Galsworthy
Gogol
Gorky (two volumes)
Harley Granville Barker
 (two volumes)
Victor Hugo
Henrik Ibsen (six volumes)
Jarry

Lorca (three volumes)
Marivaux
Mustapha Matura
David Mercer (two volumes)
Arthur Miller (five volumes)
Molière
Musset
Peter Nichols (two volumes)
Joe Orton
A. W. Pinero
Luigi Pirandello
Terence Rattigan
 (two volumes)
W. Somerset Maugham
 (two volumes)
August Strindberg
 (three volumes)
J. M. Synge
Ramón del Valle-Inclan
Frank Wedekind
Oscar Wilde

Methuen Drama Classical Greek Dramatists

include

Aeschylus Plays: One
(Persians, Seven Against Thebes, Suppliants,
Prometheus Bound)

Aeschylus Plays: Two
(Oresteia: Agamemnon, Libation-Bearers, Eumenides)

Aristophanes Plays: One
(Acharnians, Knights, Peace, Lysistrata)

Aristophanes Plays: Two
(Wasps, Clouds, Birds, Festival Time, Frogs)

Aristophanes & Menander: New Comedy
(Women in Power, Wealth, The Malcontent,
The Woman from Samos)

Euripides Plays: One
(Medea, The Phoenician Women, Bacchae)

Euripides Plays: Two
(Hecuba, The Women of Troy,
Iphigeneia at Aulis, Cyclops)

Euripides Plays: Three
(Alkestis, Helen, Ion)

Euripides Plays: Four
(Elektra, Orestes, Iphigeneia in Tauris)

Euripides Plays: Five
(Andromache, Herakles' Children, Herakles)

Euripides Plays: Six
(Hippolytos, Suppliants, Rhesos)

Sophocles Plays: One
(Oedipus the King, Oedipus at Colonus, Antigone)

Sophocles Plays: Two
(Ajax, Women of Trachis, Electra, Philoctetes)

For a complete catalogue
of Methuen Drama titles
write to:

Methuen Drama
36 Soho Square
London W1D 3QY

or you can visit our website at:

www.methuendrama.com